\# 15

D0556885

Copernicus

Struggle and Victory

by

Heinz Sponsel

translated by

Monica Gold

Printed with support from the Waldorf Curriculum Fund

Published by:

The Association of Waldorf Schools
of North America
3911 Bannister Road
Fair Oaks, CA 95628

Title: *Copernicus: Struggle and Victory*
Author: Heinz Sponsel
Translator: Monica Gold
Editor: David Mitchell
Illustrator: Wilhelm Pretorius
Proofreader and copyeditor: Ann Erwin
Cover: Hallie Wootan
© 2004 by AWSNA
ISBN # 1-88836559-5
Originally published in Germany by Meissners Books for Youth, Otto
   Meissners Publisher / Castle Bleckede on the Elbe,1949
Printing House: Hans Kock, Bielefeld

Note: Otto Meissners Verlag was shut down after World War II and
Heinz Sponsel is a pseudonym. The translator and editor have made
considerable but unsuccessful efforts to contact the heirs. We welcome
any information that help us make a connection.

TABLE OF CONTENTS

Nikolaus Copernicus

Foreword

Nikolaus Copernicus
Cleric and Astronomer
1473–1543

Finally we shall place the Sun himself at the center of the Universe. All this is suggested by the systematic procession of events and the harmony of the whole Universe, if only we face the facts, as they say, "with both eyes open."

— Copernicus from
De Revolutionibus Coelestibus

Alanus Ab Insulis gave an imagination to his students in the school of Chartre, where he pointed to the fact that Christianity would be renewed when the dark age of Kali Yuga concluded. Living in the twelfth century, he told a small circle of his closest students,

Today, we still look at the world with the Earth at the center. We judge everything from the Earth alone. If this would continue the earth evolution would not be able to progress. We have to make an agreement with the Aristoteleans who bring to mankind the intellect which then in the twentieth century must be spiritualized and bring a new light to man. We now see the Earth as the center of the cosmos, if we see the planets circling around the Earth, we describe the whole starry sky as if everything circles around the Earth, but there will still be someone who comes and places the Sun into the center. Then the prevailing worldview will become barren. People will talk about the stars as if they were just made of gaseous substances, which burn and enlighten the sky. They will understand the heavens only through their calculations. This barren worldview will spread, but it has one tiny spark: We look at the world from the earth; but one who will come [Nikolaus Copernicus] who will see the world from the Sun. He will be someone who only points in the direction—the direction of a magnificent and important path which embodies the most beautiful happenings and the most sublime beings. He who comes, however, will give only the abstract path. The world must become a desert with wonderful monuments because in the spiritual world is someone who will, together with the new intellectuality, point the path to a new spirituality, and he is Saint Michael. The field must become free for him, so that he can sow new seeds. For this reason there may be nothing but a line, a mathematical line!

Monica Gold remembered this book from her childhood in Germany. As a youth it made a profound impression on her, from both the content of the biography and the spiritual awakening it evoked. It was with joy that she undertook this wonderful translation to share with children everywhere.

— David Mitchell
Boulder, 2004

1

MYSTERIOUS SIGNS

The sun stood high in the summer sky above the city. The winding alleys and streets in the city of Torun, Po land, were deserted. Houses with steeply gabled roofs had their window shutters tightly closed so that the unbearable heat of the early afternoon could not penetrate into the rooms of merchants and traders. All around the city golden yellow fields stretched far into the distance, their grains ready for harvesting. Wagons laden with the autumn harvest stumbled with screeching wheels over the bumpy road. Between its riverbanks the waves on the broad Vistula seemed slow and lethargic, yet one could sense the closeness of the sea to which it made its way. Here and there a slight breeze could be felt as it brought salty air from the north to the peaceful city.

Many boys caught the sun as they lay on the hot, soft sands by the riverbank. They lay with their sunburned arms crossed under their heads and dreamed into the blue sky and into the few white clouds which sailed high above them. Younger ones built the most daring mountains with water, sand and stones. They destroyed them with a quick movement of their hands when they no longer liked them and began new creations. When the sun burned their skin too strongly they jumped up and ran laughing into the cool, yellow water. With arms and legs whirling, they splashed in the water so that the white foam sprayed all around them, covering their slim bodies with silver rays. Joyfully and full of laughter, they played until they were tired. Then, carried by the river's waves, they found their way back to the bank.

Once again they stretched themselves out on the hot sand, closed their eyes and began to dream new dreams.

Among them was Nikolaus Copernicus. His eyes were almost closed as he listened to the murmuring of the waves. There was nothing on the river as far as he could see. By the river's edge, a few boats were dancing up and down, firmly chained to posts. As the chains rattled against the posts he became aware of the high masts among them. The colorful sails of red, blue and white were not to be seen because they were stashed away at the bottom of the boats; the ropes, however, vibrated softly in the wind. Nikolaus turned his head and looked at the familiar picture of his hometown with its towers and gates. Then he reclined again into the sand and felt its beautiful warmth radiating from the small grains. He closed his eyes to the glistening rays of the sun as it wandered like a golden ball across the wide sky.

"Nik! Nik!"

The young Nikolaus felt two strong fists jog him into consciousness. He rubbed his eyes and forehead with his hands, trying to shake off his lethargy.

"Nik! The boats are coming!"

Immediately he was wide awake, and jumping up he ran with the rest of the boys to the river's edge. Very far away, where the river Vistula makes a big bend, a few dark points were floating on the water. Slowly they became more visible, wider and more majestic. As they watched, the boys could begin to make out the structures and railings that were erected on and around the decks of the boats. Now the deep, heavy sounds of the ship-bells interrupted the quiet of the afternoon in Torun, telling all the inhabitants that seafarers had returned from a long, dangerous journey. The jubilant shouts of the young boys mixed with the sounds of the bells, becoming a powerful chorus of rejoicing which penetrated the city and its fields. Hands were lifted in order to wave across the water to the tanned sailors, who stood with laughing faces as they returned the greeting.

Following the ships, the boys, filled with excitement, ran along the riverbank shouting loudly as they tried to keep up with the boats. They jumped through Nun's Gate and Sailor's Gate, turned around at the Ferry Gate and waited breathlessly on the quay of Torun's harbor. They watched as the well-trained men in charge of steering turned mighty wheels to carefully guide the boats along the harbor wall for safe anchoring. The wet ropes fell onto the cobblestones and were fastened by experienced hands around iron posts. The waves stormed high up against the bows of the ships and splashed their waters over the landing. It was like wonderful rain from a cloudless sky. Then the boats became almost motionless as they came to rest in their own familiar harbor. The carved names of the ships were lit up by sunlight; pennants from strange lands and cities hung on the masts and served as proof of a long journey successfully completed. The sails were taken in and the ships' gangways were pulled over to firm ground. Slowly the ringing of the bells died down. Now many busy hands began to unpack boxes and barrels. They opened bundles, which carried precious valuables from many different countries. Torun's merchants had waited for this moment through many a sleepless night. It was important to check the goods, make an inventory, describe and appraise them so that they could soon be sold to other merchants all over the country. Then the empty storage spaces could once again be filled.

Unable to help, the boys knew they were just in the way. They began to jog back down from the harbor to their bathing place at Nun's Gate. They would return to the boats when all the goods were unloaded in order to explore the cabins, look at the masts and take in the smells of far away lands. They stopped often to look back at the boats, as though invisible hands were drawing them to the many mysteries connected with these ships, secrets that they could only imagine.

Nik and his older brother Andrew turned uphill from the river at Ferry Gate. They ran through St. Anne's Alley, past the house in which they were born and into the market. They walked around the church of St. John with its big, grand tower and crossed the street by the old town hall. Its richly decorated rooftop glistened in the sunlight. They stood before the beautiful house with its impressive vaulted entranceway on which was written their father's name in heavy lettering: "Nikolaus Copernicus, Merchant."

They wanted to be present when their father entered the courtyard with his heavily laden carriage, ready to unpack and store the newly-acquired goods. It was a special hour when the unknown vastness of the world appeared before their eyes, when they saw strange names on boxes and bales, names they were unable to pronounce. It was a moment when they experienced more strongly than at any other time that the real world began, beyond the place where Torun's last houses stood, where the Vistula disappeared around a bend. They felt that there must be many other stars that they had never seen, stars of which they could only dream.

That night Nikolaus could not sleep. It was not the heavy moist air of the summer night that prevented him closing his eyes, but a longing that he could not describe. The room he shared with his brother Andrew suddenly felt unbelievably narrow. The wooden chandelier with six candles that hung from the ceiling was transformed into a magnificent ship full of secrets and adventures of an unknown world. Only the stars were the same as every other night, shining through the open window, and the pale moon was in its first quarter.

Nik listened into the dusky room. He could hear only the deep regular breathing of his brother. The entire house was silent. There was not a sound coming from the room where his two sisters, Barbara and Catherine, were sleeping. His parents too had gone to bed a while ago. Not a beam of light fell into the courtyard from any of the rooms. Nik knew that he alone was still awake. With wide-open eyes he lay in his bed, and his thoughts ran away with him down to the anchored ships on the river Vistula. Soon the boats would be ready to leave for a new journey with new adventures.

Suddenly he got up; he was no longer able to stay in his bed, nor in his room. He put on his trousers and jacket and found his sandals. For a while he stood by the window undecided, a little afraid, then feeling his courage. The window was almost at ground level and led into the yard. Once more he listened, bending forward. He could not hear a sound, only his heart beating more strongly than usual; it was joy and fear. Satisfied he nodded his head, and then lightly and carefully swung himself over the windowsill and slid into the courtyard. He had to find his way carefully between high towers of boxes and bundles. He climbed onto a huge barrel and stood on top of it like a victorious statue, then readied himself for a jump to the street. He was swallowed by the darkness. Just able to see the figure of the night watchman disappearing behind the great tower of St. John's Church, Nikolaus pressed himself into the shadow of the wall, afraid that someone might have heard his landing on the cobblestones. He felt his heart beating wildly and almost regretted following his longing. But when he looked up at the stars and felt their quiet radiance, he became quiet and all fear was gone.

He walked the well-known path through the sleeping city of Torun, across the market place and through the alley of St. Anne. He found his way through the dark arch of Ferry Gate, where his footsteps sounded so terrifyingly loud and hollow that once again he was seized by fear. But when he heard the murmuring waters of the river, again he was calmed and a thousand enemies storming towards him could not have frightened him. The black hulls of the ships stood out like ghosts against the background of the harbor wall. The high masts stretched like black fingers towards the sky. On the bows the gloomy lamps bobbed slowly up and down. The candles in the storm lanterns were mirrored by the waves.

Nik still moved in the protective shadow of the storage elevator and the warehouses that stood next to the harbor wall. He looked down at the tied ships, one fastened next to the other. In the moonlight he tried hard to decipher their names painted in light colors on the bows. "*Hanse*," he read and, "*God of the Seas – Krakow – Madonna*." His lips moved without a sound. He walked a few steps further on and breathed a sigh of relief when he discovered the name he was looking for:

"*Silesia*," he murmured and again: "*Silesia*."

It sounded like a secret prayer. Yes, there lay his ship, almost at the end of the harbor wall, the last in the long row of mute boats. Somewhere down in its bowels slept the old Kirsten in his small cabin. Kirsten and his father had been friends for many years. Both of their ancestors, like most of Torun's inhabitants, had come many years ago from Silesia in order to live and work here. His father and the seafarer Kirsten were especially connected because their ancestors had emigrated from the little village Koeppernig by the river Neisse.

Nik was wondering whether the old Kirsten would still remember the whistle which they had agreed upon many weeks before this last journey. Quietly, he tried to see if he could still do it; the whistle was not easy, and none of the city boys could imitate him. Nik pursed his lips and then he nodded his head with satisfaction. He so much wanted Kirsten to tell him about foreign countries and different cultures. He wanted to hear about storms at sea, far away cities, and of strange fish and stars not seen around where the river Vistula flows.

Quietly Nik crept to the iron post to which the boat "Silesia" was anchored with thick ropes connecting it to the riverbank. The waters gurgling deep down washed around its bow. Nik almost felt dizzy as he moved closer to the wall. Looking down into the water his mirror image seemed dark and mysterious. A few sea gulls passed silently very close by him as they flew through the night and settled on the railing.

Nik whistled, timidly at first, as if he were afraid to violate the silence, then he repeated the strange melody a little louder. It sounded like an old folk tune. He heard a dog's muffled growl, then footsteps shuffling across wooden beams. They stopped. For a third time Nik's whistle sounded through the air. Then Nik heard the echo, the same melody, and he knew Kirsten had heard him. Again footsteps shuffled through the night, and a figure appeared hastening across the deck up to the point of the bow. If Nik had any doubt that this shadow really belonged to Kirsten, the sight of the man who stood across from him now, with his square shoulders and his long white beard, took away any remaining uncertainty.

"Nik?" The question came from the ship, slowly and full of astonishment.

"Kirsten! Yes, Kirsten!" Nik was jubilant. He had to be careful not to shout out his joy in the silence. Moments later the gangway was pulled over to reach the harbor wall.

"Well, come aboard!"

Quickly Nik jumped onto the narrow, bouncy plank and then helped Kirsten pull it back onto the boat. He stood up next to the mighty shadow of the seafarer.

"In the middle of the night?"

Nik was silent.

"Do your parents know about this?"

Nik bowed his head.

"And when they miss you, boy?"

There was still no answer from the fugitive. Suddenly as Nik thought of the consequences of his nightly escapade, all his unbounded joy evaporated and became overshadowed by pressing fear. He listened to Kirsten mumbling something into his beard and did not know whether it was praise or blame.

"Come with me, and quickly!"

Nik could not do anything else. He pressed the man's hand. He wanted to say something but could not utter a single word.

They squeezed through a narrow trap door and onto a steep ladder; which took them down into the bowels of the ship. They walked along a corridor that smelled of many things: cod liver oil, spices, tobacco and the sea. They entered a small cabin.

Kirsten lit a large, round candle and clumsily sat down on a circular bench by a low table. Decorating the walls were masks with contorted faces grinning down at Nik, and for a moment he felt terrified.

"Are you afraid of these masks, Nik?" The seafarer laughed. "Be content that you did not meet the islanders where the masks came from. You are young and they would have liked your tender flesh better than my old hard bones!"

Kirsten's loud laughter shook his body and it took a long time before he was able to continue talking. Then he told the boy who was breathlessly listening all about the journey just completed. Nik lived through storms and dangers, overcome only through miracles. He saw before him peoples from different and unknown countries; mountains appeared, mountains whose tops nobody had ever seen because they stretched so far into the heavens. The narrow walls of the small cabin opened up and a magic world emerged before him: slim palm trees from which monkeys skilfully threw coconuts; animals that could swallow people whole; a burning, hot sun which mercilessly scorched everything; and deserts in which one found nothing but sand.

Motionless, Nik crouched on the bench next to Kirsten and his desire to explore the unknown burned more strongly than ever; the unknown in earth and sky. How he envied the old sea captain! And to him it did not seem difficult to explore the unknown. One needed only courage and a strong will!

Suddenly Kirsten interrupted his stories, got up, and from a small, locked cupboard in the wall took out a paper. It was beautifully folded and, as he began to open it up with infinite care, he became more pensive. He handled the paper awkwardly. It was as though his clumsy fingers and strong hands were afraid of experiencing pain, or being the cause of irreparable damage to the valuable script. He moved the light quite close to the unfolded paper so that the candle illuminated it. Nik moved even more closely in beside Kirsten and stared at the strange symbols, which he could see but which did not make any sense to him. He wanted to ask a question, but when he lifted his head and looked at Kirsten's face, he realized that he had never seen him like this before. He had become quite reverent; was he praying? Nik waited in silence for Kirsten to begin his explanation.

"Do you understand this, Nik?" the old one asked the question slowly, almost a whisper.

The boy shook his head.

"It is a great secret, Nik, a very great secret, and there are only a very few people who know about it."

Kirsten was absorbed as he looked at these symbols. It was as if he had to remember the meaning of all he saw.

"It was in Egypt, Nik, in the land of the Sphinx and the pyramids. There I received this parchment. An old, wise man revealed its secrets to me."

"Egypt?" asked Nik without understanding what he was saying.

"Far down in the south you will find this country. One has to sail for many weeks, and it is a dangerous journey."

Kirsten bent low over the paper and his mighty head cast a strong shadow over the pictures, drawn by the hand of a stranger.

"There are twelve star signs Nik, and the fate of every human being is hidden in these images. One only needs to know how to read them. The old, wise Egyptian taught me this magic art. Twelve star signs, Nik!"

Nik saw how Kirsten moved his finger from picture to picture and heard how he murmured something for each one. Motionless the boy tried to understand.

"Aries, Taurus and Gemini. Cancer, Leo, Virgo, Libra, Scorpio and Sagittarius. Capricorn, Aquarius, and Pisces."

There was silence in the cabin. Only the waters of the Vistula could be heard lapping against the ship. Nik stared at the paper, scared by what he saw and felt. Was this a magician sitting next to him? In the end curiosity and thirst for knowledge were stronger in the boy than the fear which threatened to overwhelm him. The images he saw on the paper were meant to depict stars! He thought about what the old man had said, that every single human fate was hidden in these drawings, but his mind could not grasp it.

Kirsten's voice interrupted his thoughts:"When were you born Nik?"

"1473."

"The year is not enough. I need to know the month and you have to tell me the exact day!"

"On February 19th."

"February 19th." Kirsten repeated quietly, and again he mumbled: "On February 19th."

Then he laid his finger on one of the signs and turned the candle in such a way that its light shone on it. Nik gazed at the picture that looked like two fish.

"F - f - ish?" the boy asked shyly and with a stutter.
Kirsten looked at him in surprise, and then laid a hand on Nik's shoulder:

"Yes, Nik, two fishes. Your stars are in the sign of the fish, and I believe the Egyptian said these stars are good stars. They lead man on a long, hard road. At the end of the road the sun will shine more brightly than before."

Kirsten folded up the parchment just as he had opened it, and for fear of harming it placed it tenderly and with care back into the wall cupboard. He then quietly locked it. He held the boy by the hand: "It is time for you to go, Nik! Midnight passed long ago."
He accompanied Nik back the same way onto the deck, pulled the gangway over to the quay and silently waited as the boy left the ship. In the middle of the plank high above the gurgling water, Nik stopped and turned around; suddenly he felt dizzy.

"What is wrong, Nik?"

"Kirsten, please give me the drawings as a gift!"

The old man stood there silently, just shaking his head.

"Or please, copy the pictures for me!"

"I can neither draw nor write, Nik!"

The boy became sad, he turned and walked the rest of the way onto the quay. At the harbor wall he stopped once more:

"When I have learned to draw, may I copy the pictures?" Nikolaus asked.

"Nik, your stars are in the sign of the fish, according to the old Egyptian, and I believe that later on you will not need my drawings. You will walk a steeper road, and brighter than all the stars together, the one and only sun will shine for you!"

Nik still wanted to say something. But when he looked back, he was surrounded by darkness. Far, far in the east the sky began to lighten.

"The sun rises!" he thought.

"The sun!"

Then the sleeping city and its many alleyways engulfed him.

2

THE SUNDIAL ON THE TOWER OF LESLAU

I n the small city of Leslau by the river
Vistula, the bright, shrill sound of a
bell was heard above the tree-encircled
yard of the cathedral school. A strict voice
was calling for order and silenced the loud
voices and happy games of many young
boys. They formed lines, always two together in their class groups, and soon disappeared through the wide, vaulted gate
into the cool passageways of the school
whose thick, stone walls kept out the humid air of the unbearably hot day. The long
rows of pupils ascended steps with richly
decorated banisters, then separated through different doors into
their classrooms. The long morning break had come to an end.

In the classroom the boys, filled with excitement and anticipation, waited in their seats . One could see from their nicely
tailored suits, made from fine cloth, that they were sons of well-
to-do families of the land. They were sent to the cathedral school
of Leslau to learn how to eventually take leading positions in the
city. There were not many schools that admitted the children of
poor people in the city or the surrounding countryside, and of
the few that had opened their doors, hardly anyone had been
successful in teaching these children how to read and write. The
majority of children did not go to school and so had to learn
what their parents could teach them. But there were many sub-

jects taught in Leslau's Cathedral school: Latin and German, mathematics and natural sciences, geography, and singing.

The tense silence in which the boys expectantly awaited the teacher was suddenly interrupted by a whisper. It began in the back row and rippled through all the rows to the front:

"Did you know that we have a new boy coming today?"

"His uncle is supposed to be the Bishop of Ermland, Lukas Watzelrode!"

"Oh, so he must be nobility!"

"Does anyone know his name?"

"He is called Nikolaus Copernicus."

Just as the whispering had begun, it died down. The door opened and Nikolaus Wodka, the mathematics teacher, entered the classroom. Closely following his footsteps was a boy. Fairly tall for his fourteen years and quite slim, he walked with insecure steps as so many unfamiliar eyes were turned on him, scrutinizing him from head to toe! The teacher approached his lectern and for a while silently surveyed his class until even the quietest sound ceased and one could have heard a pin drop. As he began to speak with a soft, subdued voice, he was clearly heard in the farthest corner of the classroom:

"Today we have a new pupil in our class, Nikolaus Copernicus from Torun. I hope that you will soon be good friends!" Then he said, "There, Copernicus, over there in the last row there is still a place for you."

Nik was in a hurry to disappear onto the suggested bench, relieved to no longer be exposed to his peers' pitiless gazes that seemed to penetrate the deepest fold of his heart. Fleetingly he looked around the classroom. Colored maps were visible all around, and the large blackboard was completely filled with a maze of bewildering lines, straight and curved, and numbers. For Nik it was dizzying. Through the window was the mighty cathedral tower that stretched far up into the sky, of which he could see only a very small part. He looked across the benches and the many unknown faces of youths and with names he did not know. But he had no time to think about whom he would like to choose as his friend; the hour-long lesson began and carried him into mysterious depths, which allowed no space for his own thinking. Nikolaus Wodka was a teacher who perceived immediately when a boy became absentminded and had stopped thinking about his lesson.

It was during one of these afternoon lessons that Nikolaus Wodka began to speak about the stars. In the sober schoolroom with its thick, stone walls, there arose a world of wonder. The eyes of all the boys were glued to the blackboard on which many pictures of stars were drawn with colorful chalk lines: the Big Dipper and the Small Bear, Orion, and the Polar Star, Mars and Venus, and the white band of the Milky Way appeared on the black slate like a silver passage. At this moment Nik remembered the mysterious discussion many years before in the narrow cabin of the Vistula ship "*Silesia*," and the bearded seafarer who sat on a low bench before a flickering candle. Nikolaus thought of Kirsten and the unfolded paper with all its secret signs lit by red candlelight. Then Nikolaus had a premonition that Nikolaus Wodka was the one to lead him further into the realm of stars, and to those stars that seemed to lie beyond all human recognition in a land so majestic that it would probably never, be totally revealed. Suddenly, as he was staring at the blackboard, he decided to look for an opportune moment to speak with his teacher about the night he had spent with Kirsten. If what the old seafarer had brought back from his journey to Egypt were true, then surely Nikolaus Wodka could reveal even greater secrets.

The morning passed by faster than ever before in the cathedral school. Nikolaus had heard by chance that every night the teacher worked high up in the tower of the cathedral and stayed awake until deep into the night in order to look at the stars and observe the sky. It was in this place that Nikolaus decided to approach his teacher in order to speak with him, and not in the schoolroom with its thick walls, which was narrow and oppressive, and where one could see only a small part of the sky. No, not in the depths, but in the expanding heights of the tower, from where one could gaze over the whole city and the river and where one could follow the sky to its farthest limits. Up there and not near the ears of his many classmates he wanted to share his story with Nikolaus Wodka, all by himself.

The opportune moment arrived one evening when all the pupils were playing happily in the cathedral yard. He separated from his peers, sneaked around the long, expansive buildings and hurried through the wrought-iron portal to the tower. Before he was able to walk confidently he needed to get used to the dim twilight. Dark and ghostlike, the heavy beams stared at him from the mighty, cracked, stone walls. Heavy bell ropes swung to and fro as if invisible hands were moving them. Here and there Nik could hear creaking sounds in the wooden pews, and with a sigh he looked up at the heights and tried to see how much further he had to go before he reached Nikolaus Wodka. He felt very uneasy in the musty tower and there were times when he really wanted to turn around and run back. In the deep recesses of the tiny stone windows squatted comical night birds, that, whenever he crept past them, lifted their heads from under their plumage, ruffled their feathers, and stared at his passing figure with unblinking eyes before sinking back into their dull, brooding positions. Nik had to summon all his courage to climb higher. He passed by the silent bells, which had figures and letters cast into their brazen mantles. He laid his hand on the bare metal of one bell and shuddered when he felt its coldness penetrate his whole body. With one finger he carefully pushed against it and perceived the delicate fine tones that no one else could hear: deep and light, dark and high, depending on the size of the bell he sounded.

Finally a steep ladder led him to the highest point, the top of the tower. He was undecided as he stood on the last rung, uncertain as to whether he dared disturb his teacher. Suddenly he banged his foot carelessly against one of the large beams, which resulted in a loud, penetrating boom. A door was flung open and Nikolaus Wodka stood in its low frame almost filling it with his broad body.

"Copernicus?" he said slowly, completely astonished.

He did not receive an answer.

"What are you searching for here in the tower?"

For a time Nik looked up at his teacher and, before he knew it, had spouted:

"The stars!"

In the depths, the echo was heard dully as it rebounded off the ancient walls of the tower:

"The stars!"

Only two words, then he bowed his head as if he were ashamed that he had exposed his innermost longing so blatantly. He wished that he had never climbed up. He even wished that he could hide beneath one of the huge bells down below, unreachable and far away; he wanted to be invisible. Again he heard his own voice for the third time. Surprised, he lifted his head, and in his words he felt there a hidden, vibrating joy:

"The stars!"

Then he noticed a hand beckoning him and the figure moved out of the way to let him in. With a quick and energetic movement he climbed the last rung, pulled himself up, entered the space and dropped the door latch.

Full of wonder he looked around the circular room. Wide windows were built into the walls, which made it possible to look in every direction. Slowly, almost solemnly he walked around the room and looked out. Down below he saw the city of Leslau as if it were a dream. The houses, that were far away, looked as if they had come out of a toy box. Tiny, almost invisible points were moving about the streets and alleyways.

"The people look like ants," he thought to himself.

The Vistula wound its way through the countryside, and the colorful dots of sails in red, blue and white shone on the loamy water:

"Ships that have sailed from Torun and beyond, then much further out to the sea, and from there still further!" he spoke to himself, with a feeling of indescribable longing for the unknown.

Then he turned away from the depth of his feelings and lifted his head to look up high, and still higher, into the sky. It came to him as a shock to see the vastness of the sky. Never in his young life had he been so close to it. He had only seen the sky from the ground before or from the green branches of a tree that he had climbed. But now, here, he felt he could grasp the stars with his hands as they emerged in this night of ever-increasing darkness.

"The stars!"

Again he was overcome by the words; they carried a magic from which he could not escape. With slightly parted lips he stared silently into the infinite expanse.

Smiling, Nikolaus Wodka observed the boy without disturbing him. He stood before a small table on which there were measuring instruments as well as many sheets of paper with confusing lines and long columns of numbers. The joy of this boy became his own joy; the boy's wonder and awe reminded him of his own experiences of many years ago. He, too, had once looked at the wonders of the sky in silent reverence. Slowly Nik moved from the window to the center of the room. He looked at the many drawings on the table, and it seemed to him as if the marks and figures were similar to those on Kirsten's map. He tried hard to recall the names he had heard during that special night so long ago. As much as he tried, he could not succeed except for one: one single sign stood out with extreme clarity, two fish that swim away from each other, one above the other.

Nik stretched his finger and pointed to the paper:

"Pisces?" he said.

Nikolaus Wodka was amazed. "Yes, Copernicus, Pisces. Who taught you this?"

Haltingly and slowly to begin with and then faster, Nik told the story which he had never disclosed to anyone before. He spoke about the unforgettable night on the ship by the harbor wall in Torun, and of the secrets that Kirsten had revealed. His cheeks glowed with excitement and his voice was carried by an emotion that he had never felt before.

When Nik had finished, the teacher stood by him in silence for a long time, deep in thought. Solemnly he laid his hand on the boy's shoulder and spoke quietly, so quietly that Nik had to listen attentively to hear the words:

"Yes, Copernicus, the old Kirsten knows a great deal. But what he told you is not certain. It is only a belief, cherished by many people, that their lives and fates, their happinesses and sorrows are connected to the star signs under which they were born."

His words were interrupted as he searched among his papers and pulled out a sheet upon which Nik could see the drawings of many confusing circles that criss-crossed each other; he followed the lines with his fingers.

"Here! Here, my boy, you have a drawing that shows what can be calculated and proven through mathematics. Here is what many people, over many centuries, have developed together through endless nights, daytime observations and calculations. And still, it is only a very small beginning. Much remains to be done. One has to observe again and again, compare and calculate. A person will make mistakes and be disappointed and will have to start all over again. One life is too short to complete this task. Even when one is inwardly sure what is right, one can fall into error. Who knows for sure that the Earth remains static and that the Sun, Moon and the stars circle around it? Someone else could come along tomorrow who declares the opposite. And then, on another day a third person will come along and present the whole universe from an entirely different viewpoint?"

Nikolaus listened in silence. He watched the teacher drop the paper and search for a strange instrument. "What is that?" he asked, full of curiosity.

"A Parallacticum."
"A Pa –, a Palla –?" He was unable to pronounce the word, it sounded so strange.

"A Parallacticum!" Nikolaus Wodka repeated it slowly, pronouncing every syllable and letter clearly.

"P-a-r-a-l-l-a-c-t-i-c-u-m!" said Nik and breathed a sigh of relief when he managed to master the word from beginning to end without mistake.

"Bravo, Copernicus!"

"What is it used for?"

The teacher turned the strange device in his hands this way and that so that Nikolaus could see it from all sides.

"Here you see a tripod and here is a kind of visor. When you look through this visor you can see and calculate the angle between the horizon and the star which you observe."

The teacher put the instrument back on the table and, one by one, looked at other instruments strewn among the papers.

"This one here is called a Astrolabe, and here you see a Quadrant. There on the wall next to the door hangs a Triquatum."

Nik looked at his teacher with ever widening eyes, so much so that Nikolaus Wodka had to laugh. But quickly he became serious again and said:

"Here you are, not even an hour in my observatory, and I want to teach you everything which took me years to learn. No, Copernicus, I should remember that it does not go as speedily as we might wish. But now you know where you can find me in the evenings, and I want you to know that I would be delighted if you will visit me in my dizzy-making hideaway. Of course it will be only when you feel like it, and when you do not want to play with your friends in the cathedral yard."

Then he lit a candle, took Nikolaus's hand, and opened the door for him and shone the light as the boy climbed down the steep ladder. The shadows of the bells fell long and heavy over the wall, and the strong ropes which were lit became like golden rays in the dark tower.

Only when Nik was half way home did he remember that he had completely forgotten to thank Nikolaus Wodka.

"I will come back! Oh yes, every night I will be back to visit you and the stars!" he whispered to himself as he walked along, and then he began to whistle. It was a happy tune that sounded through the dark town. It was a song he always whistled when he felt very happy, but he did not know whether the tune would reach all the way up to the uppermost tip of the Cathedral of Leslau, and the mysterious room, full of a thousand secrets that lay beyond the seam of the sky. It was a very important moment for him because he realized that he had fallen passionately in love with the stars, the Sun, and the Moon just like the lonely scientist had, who was now high above the multitude of colorful, city houses.

ᵷ   ᶚ   ᶐ

Weeks and months passed by like the ebb and flow of waves of the Vistula's yellow, murky waters. There was hardly an evening when Nikolaus did not take his beloved walk across the school yard to the cathedral, and from there, climb up the steps to the heights. He began to feel an uncertainty about the sun, moon and stars, and the knowledge that patient people had wrestled with and acquired over centuries. He had a premonition of how infinitely expansive the questions were that still needed to be considered. His will and ambition to help bring more light into the darkness welled up in him, even if it was only to be a very small light with which he was going to illumine that darkness.

One day on a free afternoon, Nik sat in the cathedral school's inner courtyard under the shady arches. He was looking dreamily into a clear fountain, whose water pipe spouted a forceful beam of water into a wide basin. He felt a hand on his shoulder and turned around. Behind him stood Nikolaus Wodka, very serious.

"Would you like to help me, Copernicus?"

He was surprised at the unexpected question. There was something concealed in his teacher's voice that startled Nik even further, but before he could free himself from his surprise he heard the voice continue:

"I want to build a clock—so big, that all the people in Leslau will be able to see it!"

Nik's jaw dropped and his eyes opened wide. He stared at his teacher who looked as if he had just spoken about the beautiful weather rather than a plan which was inconceivable to Nikolaus.

"Come with me!"

Both crossed the inner courtyard, walked through the gate and turned towards the south side of the mighty cathedral tower. There they remained standing.

"A clock? And all of Leslau is supposed to see it?" said Nik, shaking his head. The teacher smiled wisely.

"I know you're thinking of the hourglasses in our houses and the sand that drizzles through the tiny opening from the top glass to the bottom one, and when completely empty an hour has passed. No, Nikolaus, not an hourglass. We will build together a—sun clock. A sun clock high above the city and on this tower!"

Nik watched as his teacher walked a few steps closer to the heavy wall, looked up, and nodded. He was satisfied because there was no house or high tree blocking the sky.

"Yes, here the scaffold will be erected and up there we will build the sun clock! The place is perfect and the sun shines on the wall from early lunchtime until nightfall."

With a thousand unresolved questions, anxieties and doubts, Nikolaus looked at his teacher. When he perceived the certainty that he had seen so many times in that slender face, all worries disappeared.

"Do you want to help me, Copernicus?"

For the first time in his life Nik experienced a feeling of pride. It was not a vain pride, but rather, one that gave him strength for such an unknown task. He, Nikolaus Copernicus, had been the one that was chosen even though there were many boys in the cathedral school, some of whom had received higher marks than he in certain subjects and some of whom had been there much longer than him.

"I... I...," he spoke haltingly. Then the question surfaced within him, and he demanded an answer:

"Why me?"

It was a question full of fear and joy at the same time.

"Yes, you Copernicus! Not because your uncle is the Bishop of Watzelrode. And also not because your father has passed away and I would like to help you forget your sorrow!"

"Why, then? Why me?" the boy spoke very softly.

"Many people see the sun, the moon and the stars just like you and I. But they don't think about them. You, Copernicus, love the heavenly bodies in the sky! This is the reason why I have chosen you and why I would like you to help me. We will begin tomorrow!"

From that morning on, whenever Nik was free, while his comrades played down by the riverbank or lay in the sand and dreamily followed the passing sailboats, Nik stood beside his teacher on the south side of the tower of the cathedral of Leslau. They began their work by erecting a high scaffold. The heavy beams had to be clamped together with iron clips so that summer storms would not tear them apart. In spite of these they still rocked slightly to and fro but they remained firmly fastened together. Higher and higher they built the scaffold until finally the place for the clock was reached. They covered the working area with an enormous cloth so that no one would find out what was taking place up so high.

People who walked across the square stood and asked questions but none of them were answered. Nik's friends tried to find a solution to the riddle with ever new tricks and persistent cunning. Not one of them had an inkling of what was going on above in the towering heights. Teacher and pupil had united in a secret oath that no one else should know about what was taking place. Only when the hour came for the cloth to be removed, the scaffolding taken down, and all the work finished would the people of Leslau be allowed to stand before and look up to see the great work.

The work took many days, and always the teacher and his pupil could be found on the high scaffolding.

It was on a clear, cloudless Sunday when the sun sent down burning rays from the sky that the gates of the cathedral were swung wide open and the people streamed out of the cool darkness of the interior and into the glistening light which spread across the square. A slight wind carried the sounds of the last chords of the cathedral organ across the city and out into the countryside.

Suddenly the faces of many, festively-dressed people turned towards the cathedral tower, the south wall of which had for so long been hidden by the scaffolding. It reached up into the sky once more, free to display its majesty.

Glued to the spot the crowd stared into the heights. About halfway up the tower an enormous circle had been drawn on the wall with twelve thick black numbers. Above each number was painted a strange sign. One looked like a lion, another like a bull. One resembled a scale and another showed a scorpion. Next to it was an archer; opposite it were twins, a ram, and the figure of a woman. In the center of the circle a rod came out of the wall, slightly angled and pointing to the sky; its shadow, due to the sunlight, pointed exactly to the number eleven.

The people waited, almost immoveable, in absolute awe and full of wonder as they stared up at the tower. They saw how the shadow moved on very slowly, how it reached the middle between eleven and twelve and how it approached the top number. Suddenly the four bells of the cathedral tower began to ring, interrupting the eerie silence. The sound was full and rich, filling the city and surrounding countryside, proclaiming noon. The shadow of the rod covered the number twelve exactly.

Then, just as abruptly, the melody of the vibrating bells was replaced by a single, lonely voice with a clear, strong tone that dived into every crevice of the courtyard:

"A clock! A — sun clock!"

The announcement went from mouth to mouth and reached a stupendous crescendo, as a choir with a thousand voices:

"A clock! — A sundial!"

Amidst all the people stood Nik and his teacher. They held hands, and when the many voices reached their ears, it was as though a cold shower was running down their backs. It was as if the sounds of the bells and the shouting of the masses made the sundial high up on the tower disappear into a silver fog.

They stood dumbfounded, their mouths incapable of entering into the shouts and vocal jubilation. Their lips moved only slightly, and they whispered the same words:

"A clock! — A sundial!"

For a long time these two figures stood in the sun before the tower; meanwhile all the people dispersed to their own houses. Nik and his teacher looked at the shadow that continued to move on and on, from number to number, and from figure to figure.

The sundial's construction on on the tower wall made the shadow visible for all to see.

3

IS THE EARTH A SPHERE?

It was a mild evening in the Polish city of Krakow. Towers and rooftops glowed with a rosy sheen from the setting sun. Krakow's stately castle, Wavel, with its mighty, yet clumsily built stone walls, stood on a slightly raised hill above many houses. The evening sun was casting its last rays onto the castle and shining beautifully onto the fertile valley. In the twilight one could see far away on the horizon the mountain chain of the Beskiden and High Tatra. Deep in the valley the river Vistula had its source, and it was from here that it began its tireless run of more than a thousand kilometers to the sea.

Nikolaus Copernicus was immersed in thought as he walked up and down beneath the arches and passageways that enclosed the interior court of the university. He had begun his studies here many months ago. It was Nikolaus's

uncle, Lucas Watzelrode, the Bishop of Ermland, who had enrolled him at the University of Krakow after he had promised Nik's dying father he would be responsible for his nephew's education. He had also promised that one day he would give Nikolaus the position as Canon of Frauenburg. This was the reason for sending him to this university. Its reputation was well known all over Europe, and many famous scholars had been drawn by the wide variety of subjects that were taught there:theology and law, medicine and philosophy, optical and natural sciences, and the mysteries of astronomy with its knowledge of the stars. The street where the university was located was lined with ancient trees and had the same name, Anne's Alley, as the street in Torun where Nikolaus had been born and where he had spent his early youth. This helped him to feel at home, even though he was far away in such a large and foreign city. A fountain gurgled quietly in the center of the square courtyard. The still water at its edge reflected the red of the evening sky. But Nikolaus was completely unaware of the calmness that nature was spreading around him. For days he had been tormented by an anxiety that would not leave him; it continued even into the night. Repeatedly, his thoughts wandered back to Albert von Brudzewo, the professor who gave lectures on the stars and whose name was famous across the entire Occident. From the northern sea down to Italy, from the river Vistula to Frankfurt in Germany, everywhere his name was spoken with respect and awe because there were few scientists who equaled his knowledge and dedication. In comparison to Albert von Brudzewo, even Nikolaus Wodka, his beloved and admired teacher from the cathedral school in Leslau, paled, like the flame of a candle in the glowing heat of a golden sun.

In that afternoon's lecture, Albert von Brudzewo had spoken about the Egyptian astronomer, Ptolemy, and his book which carried the mysterious title *The Almagest*. It contained the entire teaching that was known and accepted as true in the world at large. Again Nikolaus became aware of the Egyptians he had first heard of in Kirsten's ship's cabin.

He became restless; suddenly nothing could keep him any longer under the arcades of the yard. With hasty steps he climbed the wide staircase to the first floor and walked along a narrow corridor until he reached the library. The door sounded with a heavy clang as it shut. From the floor all the way up to the decorated ceiling were rows of bookshelves with many big volumes. Each tome was fastened to the wall with a thin, strong chain that could only reach as far as the nearest reading desk. Nik dili-

gently searched bookshelf after bookshelf, row after row, and
whispered a single name over and over again almost like a prayer:

"*Almagest* by Ptolemy!"

Finally he discovered the heavy book about which Albert
von Bruzewo had so often spoken. He took it from among all the
others and carried it like a relic to the desk that stood next to a
high window and through which wide rays of sunlight were flood-
ing. Feverishly he read through the lines, turning page after page.
Carefully-drawn black letters shimmered, large and majestic on
the yellow parchment.

As he became absorbed in what he was reading, everything around him seemed to disappear: the high hall with its thousands of books, the rustle of the fountain down below in its shady
court, the loud noises coming from the city streets. The whole
universe rose up before him: the earth, the sun, the moon and
stars, just as the Egyptian astronomers had foretold and which
had become the indisputable teachings of the time. Glowingly
and quietly he spoke to himself as he read these words:

"The center of the universe is the disc of the Earth, larger
than the Sun. The entire world—Sun, Moon and stars—circles
around the Earth."

The room succumbed to darkness as the night closed in
and the young student from Torun continued, bent over the famous book. He did not hear the clatter of the chains when other
people lifted books off the shelves. He lit a candle and read with
cheeks burning, feeling neither tired nor hungry nor bored. His
shadow appeared like that of a giant on the surrounding walls
as it flickered up and down in the light. He turned page after
page as one sentence after the other were engraved forever in
his memory. Once in awhile he stopped reading, propped his head
on his hands and fixed his gaze on the red-yellow flame.

Who could grasp this knowledge with its deep wisdom?
Who would be able to decipher the immeasurable secrets still

waiting to be discovered in the deepest of mysteries? How could the sun, the moon and the stars, high up in the universe, turn so restlessly? Why did they not plunge into the vast chasms of the cosmos? One question followed upon another, each becoming weightier and more important than the last. He shuddered as he stood up and thought about the many complex questions that had arisen in his mind, that even now were clamoring for answers.

"Ptolemy!"

He whispered the name and was terrified when suddenly he heard a voice calling his name and did not know where it had come from. He looked around the dusky hall but there was nobody there except himself. Only the yellowed backs of the heavy books on the shelves shimmered with a dull light. He imagined what it might be like if one day a book with his name were found among these long rows, a book in which the secrets of the world would be revealed, a book in which other young men, with fiery cheeks and glowing eyes, would turn pages just as he was doing late this evening, only he was turning the pages written by an immortal Egyptian. As he returned his attention to the book, he had to laugh at the idea, but he noticed that he could no longer concentrate on his reading. Quietly he closed the book, put it back in its place and stepped out into the courtyard, which was now completely deserted of people. He saw the first stars rising in the sky. He heard the rushing of the river, and suddenly he felt stronger and more determined than ever before.

From that evening, Copernicus sought the company of his teacher, Albert von Brudzewo, whenever possible. They walked together under the arches of the university or stood by the fountain in the center of the courtyard. Sometimes they wandered out of the city and sat by the banks of the Vistula. At night they climbed the stairs of high towers in order to see the land and the starry constellations. Wherever they were their discussions dealt with the many unresolved questions. The more difficult these questions became, the more they struggled to solve them.

During this time Nikolaus grew to love and fully trust Albert von Brudzewo. The professor was not a man interested in honors of the world, nor was he proud of his scientific achievements or reputation. He had often admitted to Nikolaus how little he knew and how long the path was to solutions.

Likewise Albert von Brudzewo had noticed that in knowledge, the merchant's son from Torun had by far surpassed his fellow students. He perceived the wisdom in all the questions Nikolaus asked, and, detected superiority in all his answers. Therefore he did not talk to Nikolaus as if he were a student but rather as he would speak to his colleagues.

One late fall afternoon the two stood, as they often did, in the large library hall. Outside, golden leaves rustled quietly as they fell from the trees; above the busy street the wide sky arched deeply in saturated blue. Nikolaus carefully closed *The Almagest* which he read almost daily, looked out of the large window and walked over to Albert von Brudzewo, who was busy drawing the planetary movements with colored chalks on a wide blackboard. For a few moments he watched him, then suddenly, and without any hesitation, he pointed to the book on the desk and exclaimed:

"The greatest book in the world!"

Albert von Brudzewo finished the drawing of a sphere, placed the chalk on the wooden sill of the board, and turned to Copernicus.

"Which book do you mean?"

"*The Almagest* by Ptolemy!" he answered in a voice whose tone expressed astonishment and displeasure at such a question. "Did you, yourself not call the book great?"

The teacher remained silent and did not confirm this sentence with a single word or a gesture of head or hands. He paced up and down between the high bookshelves that reached up like a dark wall, as if he were searching for a book. Then he pulled out a fat, yellowed volume bound in swine's leather. Thoughtfully, almost testing, he held it in his hands, undecided whether he should open it or place it back on the shelf. As he moved back to the board with the book, he answered his student:

"I have called it great, Nikolaus, but not the greatest."

"Not the greatest?" Nikolaus repeated the sentence. He felt as though this remark, spoken without compassion and with cold assertion, had shattered a world for him.

"The book has mistakes!"

Clear, and with authority, the words sounded through the room. "Mistakes!" echoed the walls of the room.

"Mistakes!" whispered the wind outside as it blew through the trees.

Copernicus felt, that with this monstrous statement coming from his beloved, yet at this moment almost hated, teacher, the ground was giving way under his feet and the earth was coming to an end.

"Mistakes?" screamed the young student, shocked by the force of his own voice.

Albert von Brudzewo stood next to the blackboard. He was totally calm and showed the superiority of a man who had gone through life having overcome many a disappointment. Quietly he waited until the storm in Nikolaus abated, then he continued in a softer voice:

"It is a fact that the theory about the Moon is incorrect."

Copernicus walked with slow, measured steps to one of the windows and looked down on the city. The golden sun and many colored leaves on the autumn trees for him turned a dull gray, without any joy or hope. He placed his hands over his ears so that he would not hear the happy singing of people in a neighboring house. He cursed the chirping of the birds in the branches and longed for a deep sleep in which he could forget everything: Albert von Brudzewo, Ptolemy, the sun, the moon and the stars, in fact the whole universe with its endless questions.

When he walked slowly back to the professor, he found him opening the book that he had been holding in his hands all this time. Curiously, he looked at the first page and read:

"*The Heavens* by Aristotle."

Albert von Brudzewo searched for a while through the pages, and then he read aloud:

"It will still be necessary to point out where the Earth is positioned, whether she is fixed or moving and what her form is."

Immobile, the professor stood by the blackboard. It was difficult for him to shatter the student's security in which he had lived up to this moment and to destroy the trust in the teachings of the Egyptian. It had become so quiet in the room that one could have heard the sand falling in an hourglass. But Albert knew that this hour had to come and he trusted that Nikolaus would find the strength to overcome the challenge. Only by knowing uncertainty could the new arise, new cognitions and new answers to age-old questions. "This is not all that I have to tell you today, Copernicus!" With resolve the student's face was turned to the professor. Pain and curiosity were mixed in his motionless expression.

"The Greek Pythagoras taught, in as far back as 500 BC, that the Earth is a sphere like the Sun, the Moon and the stars, and not a disc. Heaven does not arch like a bell over the Earth, but is an immeasurably large global vault in which all the stars revolve around the tranquil Earth."

"The Earth not a disc but a sphere?" whispered Copernicus, shaking his head. He was unable to grasp this sentence with all its sinister meaning. He had heard too much in too short a time.

"This is still not the last thing I have to tell you this afternoon."

The student's eyes were fixed on the professor's mouth and stared at his face as though he were a vision from another, unreal and ghostly world.

"In 300 BC Aristotle maintained that the Sun is the center of the universe. The Earth in the course of a year circles around the Sun, and once every day she revolves around her own axis!"

"Everything revolves around the Sun?" stammered Copernicus and then repeated the sentence once more:

"Everything revolves around the Sun?"

It seemed to him as if he the ground had gone from under his feet. The many rows of books became blurred before his eyes. Everything that was around him transformed into a foggy sea that floated up and down without boundaries.

Then he straightened himself up, and lifting his head, grew to almost beyond the professor's height. His hands became fists and deep wrinkles appeared in his face. He moved very close to Albert von Brudzewo, so close that he could feel his breath. With a hoarse voice he spoke:

"Why did you conceal all this from the public in your lectures? Why may we not know that the Earth is perhaps a sphere and that the Earth is not in a fixed position but the Sun? Why are the names of Pythagoras and Aristotle not spoken about? Why is it that only Ptolemy's teachings are reaching the world? Why? Why?"

Albert von Brudzewo stood unmoved before the anguished student. Perhaps his face had become a little paler, but the accusations of the student from Torun did not seem to touch him. Only his mouth twitched painfully when he soundlessly gave the answer to the many questions:

"The Church has forbidden it, Copernicus!"

Nikolaus was terrified upon hearing this answer. He had expected everything else but not this. He looked for words, but he was unable to express what he felt.

"To you, Copernicus, I spoke about this as the only one among many students. I did so because I knew that eventually you would read about it in old books, because you are not one of those who feels satisfied with the research others have done. You are one of those who does not give up; you will always try to get to the root of a question in order to understand. You will neither halt nor rest until you have found the truth."

Nikolaus interrupted the professor:

"Truth? Why does the Church forbid the truth?"

"The Church does not forbid the truth, you can research it as profoundly as you like. However, the church places the Earth in the center of the world because on Earth lives man, who was redeemed by Christ. The other heavenly bodies are only hot or cold stone. Do you feel now that the Earth must remain in the center, Copernicus? Thanks to your uncle you are destined to become a canon. So you too may never believe anything other than this: the Earth is a disc and everything revolves around her: Sun, Moon and stars."

"And if it could be proven that the Sun is the center, Albert von Brudzewo? And what if I could be successful in proving this? If this were the new truth?"

"It would be a dangerous truth for you, Nikolaus. It would be very dangerous to speak about it!"

The professor stepped closer to Copernicus in an attempt to stroke his hot forehead and so help calm his emotions. He felt only thin air. Unable to speak another word, and without taking his leave, Nikolaus had stormed out of the library. The heavy door fell closed with a thunderous clang. A hollow sound was heard in the quiet house; the glass in the windows clattered. Nikolaus leapt down the stairs taking two, three or four steps at a time. With a few paces he was across the courtyard without turning back to look at the library where he knew the professor had remained. Gasping for air he stood in the street that bore the familiar name, deeply he breathed in the golden sunlight; he felt like a man who, after a long prison term in an underground vault, had thrown off his chains and was once again seeing the light of day.

He hastened through the streets and alleyways of the city. He did not notice the people who walked past him, shaking their heads as they turned in amazement to watch him disappear in the distance. He did not acknowledge any greetings that were directed towards him. He did not see the girls and women who, as always, sat in the marketplace offering for sale their white bread in colorful baskets, their butter and eggs, and their milk in stone pitchers.

Without knowing how he got there, he stepped through the wide portal of St. Mary's Cathedral. He was instantly enveloped in the dimly lit cool of the high nave and he received the silence gratefully as a blessing.

He looked at the old brown wooden prayer benches and the beautiful high columns, but there was not a sign of a single human being. He remained standing before St. Mary's altar. He had heard that it had taken the wood carver and sculptor Veit Stoss from Nuremberg twelve years to carve these figures. He became absorbed by the brilliance of this masterful work and soon believed that he was no longer looking at lifeless figures, but rather at living people, as the faces and bodies that were made of dimly shining wood appeared realistically before him.

Nikolaus had not noticed the middle-aged man standing close behind him. Only when he was quietly spoken to did he emerge from his dream; it was with surprise and astonishment that he looked into a calm, serene face which showed a unique likeness to some of the heads in the carvings before him. He had not understood what the stranger had whispered to him and was so absorbed in the altar that he did not ask him. All he could say after a while was:

"A wonderful work of art!"

For a while the man looked at him, and his face radiated happy contentment. Then he spoke with a deep clear voice:

"Twelve years is a long time, young student. A very long time! But that which is supposed to turn out for the good needs to mature in silence."

"And much patience!" Nikolaus added thoughtfully.

Amazed he observed how the stranger climbed the steps to the altar and, standing before the carved wooden figures, lifted his hands, inspected and examined each figure with trembling fingers carefully caressing their faces, bodies and garments as though he wanted to find out from this contact that they had really turned out for the best. It dawned on Nikolaus then that this stranger was no other than the creator of the work. Who else would have the courage to behave in such a way? He saw how the stranger, now no longer strange to him, came back down, stood by his side and remained quiet for a while, his head bowed, as if he had to first overcome a deep disappointment. Then he spoke:

"Twelve years! And still so many mistakes. One would have to be given the strength of a lifetime for such a work as this! One's entire life! Perhaps then, and only then, one will have come a very small step closer to the truth, young scholar!"

Slowly the man made the sign of the cross in front of his forehead, mouth and chest, bowed deeply as if he were under a great and heavy burden and with heavy steps walked through the cathedral of Saint Mary. Copernicus followed him with his eyes until the figure disappeared into the dusk under the portal. For a while his footsteps still echoed in the high brick building, then once again a sacred silence descended upon and around the columns and pillars.

Once more Nikolaus saw the afternoon sun touch the figures with a soft light and it seemed to him he would never be able to find a more perfect, more complete work of art. Shaking his head he thought of the words of the master, that this work was still imperfect.

"One long life and perhaps one will come a tiny step closer to the truth." He repeated the words to himself. His thoughts turned from the sculptures before him to the figures circling in the sky that were called the sun, the moon and the stars.

Quickly he pulled himself together and with long, hasty strides he stormed out of the cathedral. He felt moved to talk once more to the creator of this work of art. But the wide-open area around the mighty cathedral lay deserted and nowhere could he detect the man with the beautiful head and the strong but finely shaped hands, who had created this magnificent work of art. Disappointed he remained under the portal because the many questions that burned in his soul still remained unanswered. Then slowly he continued on his way.

He strolled through Florian Lane with its richly decorated drapers' halls on either side, a place where merchants sold their valuable cloths. He walked along the Vistula that was quite narrow as it flowed between its riverbanks toward his distant hometown. He recalled the words that the master Veit Stoss had spoken to him, that man must serve the truth in his life on earth, and he cherished these words like a testament. At the same time he had a premonition that it could be dangerous to serve the truth. Then he felt streaming into him a mysterious force of courage and strength, and all his fear vanished He walked on,.full of trust. The last of the sun's rays were spreading light over the castle and on the hill above the city. He knew somewhere in the myriad of houses was the university and the reading room. When he stepped through the archway into the interior court with its bubbling fountain, he spoke to himself once more the last words of the sculptor:

"The truth!"

Then he climbed the stairs, which led higher and higher. The autumn gold of the trees shimmered outside the narrow windows and set his happy face aglow.

ᛝ   ᛆ   ᛦ

In the year 1492 the late autumn with its storms had moved into the countryside. Cold winds blew from the Beskid Mountains, and the higher Tatra Mountain chain had already received its first blanket of snow.

It was on one of these evenings that Nikolaus Copernicus sat together with his friends, George Donner and Peter Tiedemann, at a small table in the student tavern of Brotherhood Lane. It was comforting warmth that penetrated the cozy room, and fiery wine glowed in the polished and elegant glasses. Various discussions hummed quiet and louder, like a beehive, in the small and crowded room.

Suddenly the door was thrown open. A cold wind swept in from the outside. Yellow leaves whirled onto the tables and fell into many a glass. Tumultuous laughter began. In the frame of the door stood a student. His hair was tangled, falling disheveled across his brow, and his eyes glowed feverishly. In his hand he waved a piece of paper like a flag. With a mighty leap he entered the room and jumped onto a table. The wine glasses tipped over, spilling their contents and shattering on the floor.

"Quiet!" he shouted.

It took awhile before he gained everybody's attention. Most of the students stood up and came to the center table crowding tightly together around it.

"What is the news?"

"War against the Turks?"

"A new Pope?"

Only slowly did the questions and the shouting subside until all eyes were on the paper and the hand that held it.

"Read it!"

"Silence!"

Then it became so quiet that one could hear the crackling of paper.

"The news is from Vienna and just arrived by courier! A Spaniard has sailed west over the great sea with three ships and found land! The man is Christopher Columbus! The land is India!"

For a moment there was nothing but a breathless silence in the tavern. Then an enormous uproar began:

"That is a lie!"

"A lie! The big ocean has no borders. The Earth is a disc!" shouted a student as he jumped onto the table attempting to grab and shred the paper into pieces. Others dragged him down.

"Show us the message!"

The paper went from hand to hand and everyone read what he had already heard.

"The news is correct. Columbus has indeed found land in the west!"

Nikolaus Copernicus held the paper in trembling hands. He wiped his forehead and burning eyes, red and inflamed from his nightly studies. Then he stood up, and with one leap, jumped onto the table screaming into the crowd:

"Do you know what this means?" He waited until everyone was quiet.

"It means that the Earth is not a disc!"

"Not a disc?" one voice laughed unpleasantly from a corner of the room. "What then, you unbelievably wise Copernicus?"

Everybody stared at the figure on the table.

"A sphere!"

"A sphere? Ha, ha, ha! A sphere?" Someone in the midst of the student crowd jeered.

"A sphere!" repeated Copernicus, and he emphasized every letter of the word loudly and slowly.

Another man jumped onto the table next to him:

"Don't you dare say that again! The Church teaches that the Earth is a disc!"

Copernicus directed his gaze calmly and determinedly towards the speaker who met it, and then lowered his head. But already someone else had yelled scornfully from another corner:

"A sphere? And the people down below on the sphere, they stand on their heads, right? Ha, ha, ha!"

Many bellowed. Copernicus had more to say, but no one paid any more attention to him. He stood alone with his thoughts, on the table in the tavern.

"A joke. To you it's nothing but a joke! Only blockheads or simpletons would believe such an idea!"

Even greater laughter filled the room at his words, so with a helpless gesture Nikolaus stepped down from the table, took his wineglass, emptied it in one big gulp and then ran out the door. Biting scorn followed him:

"Stupid!"

"Rebel!"

"Fool!"

With a thunderous noise the door of the tavern fell shut. Down the street he could still hear the jeers and laughter. The night lay ominously over Krakow. Only the stars here and there shone through the clouds, as the stormy wind whipped across the sky.

4

The Stars of Italy

In the morning haze Bologna's towers and rooftops shimmered with indescribable beauty under the Ital-ian sky. For many months now Nikolaus Copernicus had experienced the lavish beauty of the southern landscape and yet every day he enjoyed its magical power anew. In comparison, his faraway home on the river Vistula often seemed bleak, bare and cold with its short summers and frosty, winter storms, monotonous fields and the gray of immeasurable flat lands!

It was not the landscape alone that held him captive. The people in this rich, fun loving city knew how to live and did not take the problems of life too seriously and were full of joy; any homesickness that he had was soon overcome. Why should he be homesick anyway? His mother and father had lain under the meadow in these last years of the fifteenth century. The friends with whom he had played had moved like the wind in all directions.

And what about Lucas Watzelrode, uncle and Bishop of Ermland? He could only think of him with painful bitterness. This strong-willed, egocentric man had tried to force him into a career to which not one fiber of his heart felt drawn. He also was planning to make him Canon of Frauenburg one day, which Nikolaus had to admit was an elevated and honored position, yet was a profession which curbed all freedom and asked for many a sacrifice.

Lucas Watzelrode had sent him to Bologna, the city at the foot of the Apennine Mountains, to study law. It was in this subject that the University of Bologna with its many learned scholars towered above every other university in Europe. Students came here from all countries in the world to hear lectures. The collection of national costumes and cultures made a colorful picture of the streets and squares of this southern city.

Copernicus was registered in the "natio Germanorum," a German student organization. He wore the dark-hooded, long robe that reached all the way down to his heels. In the book that on its first page showed the German, double-headed crowned eagle, his name was inscribed alongside names of young sons of noble birth, sons of dukes and known scholars, as well as citizens from the middle classes—in total, a noble group of students.

The merchant son from Torun, however, was a rare presence in the lecture halls of jurisprudence. His heart drove him to the lectures of the famous astronomer, Dominicus Maria di Novara, before whom Nikolaus Wodka in Leslau and the honored Albert von Brudzewo in Krakow paled in comparison. In this scientist from Bologna, Nikolaus found a passionate striving for truth, and he admired his teacher's fearless courage to question Ptolemy's ancient theories.

Nikolaus rarely allowed a day to pass by without taking a late evening walk to his professor's house, built far outside of the city on a gently rising hill in the midst of a sea of laurel, myrtle, lavender and rosemary. Oleander bushes and lemon trees grew high up into the sky, and the marbled columns of the entrance hall shimmered like silver rays between the many colors of the rich garden. Many a night the professor and his student worked until the early morning hours on the open terrace of his house. At their feet they could see Bologna spread out with its countless lights shining from the windows. Across the fertile valley were the dark silhouettes of the Apennine Mountains. The gaze of the two people was directed towards the sky and the movements of the mysterious, heavenly bodies.

"The human eye should be able to focus more clearly, like an eagle who from dazzling heights is able to see the mouse in the furrows of the field. Then new wonders might be revealed to us, wonders which we cannot even surmise. So much faster would we reach valid conclusions in our calculations," said Dominicus Maria di Novara while rubbing his strained and painful eyes.

"A few decades ago a certain Gutenberg discovered the printing press in Mainz. Daringly, sailing boats are crossing the world's stormy seas in all directions searching for new lands. And so, might it not be possible that one day someone might think of an eyeglass or tube to drawing the stars more closely from the sky to the earth?" Copernicus asked this with such force and determination that the professor was filled with admiration.

"Perhaps you are right. Why not? One must accomplish all that is possible with the instruments that are available at any given time. It is no different for us astronomers!" complied Dominicus, and took again one of the measuring instruments that lay on the balustrade of the terrace.

A few weeks after his arrival in Bologna the learned man had given the student from Torun a task, which if he solved it correctly, could open the path to completely new discoveries. He

had chosen Copernicus for this work because the letters of rec-
ommendation from Nikolaus Wodka and Albert von Brudzewo
had sung praises most highly with regard to the young student's
knowledge of astronomy. Indeed, his first discussions with
Nikolaus had already convinced him that the teachers from Leslau
and Krakow had not exaggerated. So he asked Copernicus to
solve, through regular measurements and observations, the question as to whether the moon in its different quarters changes
size, as Ptolemy insisted, or whether the size remains constantly
the same. The Egyptian had based his entire research on the fact
that the moon changes its size.

Copernicus was shocked at the significance and gravity of
such a task, and that he was deemed worthy of such a responsi-
bility. What would happen if he proved that the Egyptian had
made a mistake in his measurements? Would not the entire world
view collapse? He began the task with such frenzy that even Dominicus Maria di Novara was surprised.

He stood almost every night on the terrace under the sky.
Only when heavy clouds moved across the land or when it was a
new moon did he have an opportunity to catch up with the many
hours of lost sleep. Otherwise he knew only one thing, to observe
and to measure, to measure and to observe, to write down ever-
new numbers and to calculate row upon row. It was like placing
stone upon stone into a mighty spiritual structure that he was
meant to build. Meanwhile his friends enjoyed themselves in the
taverns or roamed at midnight in high spirits throughout the city
streets. He stood on the terrace and could hear their happy songs,
weaving through the blossoming gardens to entice him out. Often he was tempted to throw away his measuring instruments
and papers and join the intoxicating ecstasy of freedom and happiness. Then he forced himself with superhuman strength to first
solve the task that he had been given. He knew that once he had
managed to fulfill his duty there would be no student in all of
Bologna to match his joy and ability to commit pranks. A tremendous amount of patience and persistence was required to
observe and measure again and again. The pain and exhaustion
of his own body showed him that the most important things in

the world are made up of minute details. He who shuns the small will never be able to achieve the great. Week after week, month after month passed by. Flowers blossomed and wilted, trees bore fruit and were harvested, and new buds formed on the branches. On the dark terrace of a quiet home stood a lonely man under the stars. Night after night he labored, despaired, then again found new courage. In the silence and concealment of the night sky his work was born.

Week by week his understanding grew and matured to an ever-greater clarity that Ptolemy had indeed erred. The piece of paper with seemingly endless columns of numbers proved it without a doubt, anyone willing and with the same patience and persistence could check his measurements and reach the same results. He carried the precious roll of papers under his robe as he made his way to the professor's house to place the results of his research into the hands of the one who had entrusted him with the task.

The fine granules of sand crunched quietly under his feet as Copernicus walked along the garden path. In the room above him he could see a flickering light in the window, and by the bright light of a candle he perceived the shadow image of a familiar face. The student halted on the way up the marble steps. On one hand he experienced a tremendous pride at having brought the task to a successful conclusion, but on the other he felt intimidated by what might follow as a result of the discovery encoded in black and white on the papers in his hand.

Hesitantly he pressed down the door handle and crossed the threshold. Dominicus Maria di Novara lifted his head from the parchment over which he was bent.

"Copernicus?"

His glance rested on him longer than usual, as though he were examining the one who had just entered.

"You look strangely changed today. What is wrong? Are you having problems concerning the task I entrusted to you?"

With trembling hands the student opened the robe above his chest and grasped the fat roll of papers. Without speaking he placed it on the table before Dominicus Maria di Novara.

"You don't mean to say that you have finished the work already?" Astonished the professor took the papers and hastily opened them. Then he became absorbed in the long number columns and many drawings. Occasionally he mumbled to himself something undiscernible, and here and there he took his quill to check one or other of the calculations. He forgot everything around him. Copernicus stood waiting, completely motionless in front of the table of the scientist. He felt as though he were standing before a court whose judgment was going to be inexorable: either he would be freed or condemned. However, the strong trust which he carried in his heart allowed him to look forward to the final outcome.

Outside in the gardens the night passed hour after hour. The moon rolled over the shining rooftops of Bologna. Somewhere in the valleys and gardens fountains splashed, trees rustled, and one could hear joyful singing interrupting the silence of the night. After a long, long space of time Dominicus Maria di Novara leaned back in his chair and closed his eyes. With his hands he repeatedly smoothed his forehead as though it were hurting from reading the flood of numbers. Then he breathed deeply and managed to lift himself out of the armchair. In measured steps he solemnly walked around the room, and his shadow seemed mighty and majestic on the high walls around him. Priests approaching the altar in a church would not have walked any differently. When he reached Copernicus, the professor stood still, and for a while he looked at him in silence, then lifted his hands and let them rest on the shoulders of the young student.

"Nikolaus Copernicus from Torun! You have cast the teachings of Ptolemy from the throne! The Moon remains the same size in all its phases!"

With a cutting voice he spoke the judgment quietly and almost hoarsely. Suddenly the joy left his pale face and a dark and profound earnestness spread across his lips and within his eyes as he continued to speak:

"Do you realize what your calculations mean?"

He directed his gaze to the top of the table that was covered with papers in total disarray. Calmly and without any emotion Copernicus stood before Dominicus Maria di Novara. A long time ago he had asked himself the same question and found the answer. He did not have to think for very long.

"Our entire picture of the world is incorrect because it rests on the teachings of Ptolemy!"

The professor was amazed at how the student was able to speak this colossal and daring sentence so deliberately and in such a matter-of-fact way. He took him by the shoulders and shook him.

"A dangerous word, Copernicus! A far too dangerous word! You know that the Church ..."

"The Church, too, has to accept this, Dominicus Maria! Sooner or later!"

"They could bring you to Court!"

"I will fight for the truth!"

The professor was shocked when he perceived the foreboding fire that flared in the eyes of his student and when he heard in the voice an icy cold determination.

"What are you planning to do, Copernicus?"

"Everywhere I will publish and talk about this truth. The view of the world that we have relied on as regards the Earth, the Sun, the Moon and the stars is wrong!"

"But the people, Copernicus, you will tear from their hearts a centuries-old belief. Can you fill the void? Can you replace the old belief with a new one? Can you give them a true picture of the world?"

Copernicus was silent, lost in thought as he looked into the light of the candle that was almost out. Suddenly he felt tired, incredibly tired. He wanted to speak, but not a single word could he bring past his burning lips. His body, which for far too long had done without sleep, began to sway—he felt weak. The demand of many weeks and months on his strength had taken its toll.

Slowly Copernicus turned around and with a breathless farewell slipped out of the room. He did not know whether the professor had heard his departing words. He staggered down the marble steps and in a delirium walked through the scented gardens and along the now, almost invisible path. The question, which Dominicus Maria di Novara had asked remained without answer. The lonely, exhausted wanderer had a premonition that he had to journey still further along the road, not knowing when, or if, it would reach its final goal.

For a little while he sat down on a bench under an olive tree and looked down on the towers and cupolas of Bologna. The immeasurable starry sky arched over the city. For the first time Copernicus experienced a wave of homesickness. He dreamed of Torun and the Vistula, of colorful sails on large boats, red, blue and white. He had not written to his siblings for a long time! He wondered if they thought of him as proud and conceited because he was destined to become a canon and because he was able to study all this wisdom at the most famous university in Europe. With some effort he got up from the bench and walked quickly down to Bologna passing through the many narrow and wide streets of the sleeping city.

After he closed the door to his room in the German student home, he dipped his quill into some ink and began to write. This time it was not numbers that covered page after page, but sentences dictated by his heart and meant only for his siblings. These letters did not take him long to write and he was soon finished. However, the letter he wanted to write to Lucas Watzelrode had to be thought out more carefully. What was he supposed to write to his strict uncle, the mighty Bishop of Ermland? He would not want to hear about astronomy, and the lectures on jurisprudence were far too dry and dull, so there was nothing for him to say. In spite of this he knew his uncle had made it possible for him to study all these years. The inheritance left by his mother and father was small, and was shared among the four children; it would not have paid for the extensive traveling that he had undertaken. Nikolaus was grateful to his uncle, and so, in the last letter he wrote that evening, he tried to express this feeling.

The early morning light was rising above the Apennine mountain tops when Copernicus finally dried the ink with the sand shaker and placed the quill back into its glass inkstand. The first sounds of the new day were coming from the garden: birds were singing and carriage wheels bumped through the streets of the city. Heaven and earth were awakening from the healing peace. Nikolaus, however, in his total exhaustion was in a deep, dreamless sleep that lasted many, many hours.

He gave himself only a few days and nights of well-earned rest. Then once again he longed for his measuring instruments and paper.

"Whomsoever is smitten by the stars will never be let go of again!" he said to his comrades, during these nights in taverns, drinking sweet, dark red wine. Thus he spoke to the dark-haired girls with whom he wandered arm in arm through blossoming gardens, laughing and full of delight in the joy of the city. Not one of them could say that he had become a low-spirited person because of his interest in the stars.

After these days of recuperation, Nikolaus was once again in the beautiful house of Dominicus Maria di Novara. The professor, without speaking, took two glasses from a cupboard, placed them on the table between a protractor and a setsquare and filled them with bubbling wine. Before drinking he took the student by the shoulders and walked him out onto the terrace. Deep clouds had formed and blown over the land and city.

"It is not a good night," Copernicus spoke softly. "One cannot see the stars."

"Hey, Nikolaus, that is similar to us. Sometimes we think we are close to our goal, our knowledge grows, thanks to what we have discovered, which in turn results in our taking steps further forward up to this moment where you give the world a new teaching about the Moon. And yet there still exists much darkness before the light can change it into a bright clear day!"

Then he lifted the glass and said:

"To Nikolaus Copernicus!"

And he drained the glass to the last drop. The student knew that this was the greatest praise that his teacher could give him. Almost ashamed he took his glass and replied to the toast:

"To Dominicus Maria di Novara!"

He also emptied the glass with one long draught. It was like a secret conspiracy between the two lonely people high above the city, and the beginning of many new hours of observing and calculating.

On one of these nights someone knocked at the door of the room under the terrace in which teacher and student sat involved in their calculations. Astonished they looked at each other because they were not expecting anyone to find his way to them, nor did they want a visitor because he would only disturb them in their work. Before either of them could answer the knock, the door was swung open. A gust of wind blew into the room. Thunderstruck Nikolaus saw his brother's figure standing in the frame of the door. His face aglow, his clothes torn and tattered by the long exhausting journey: from the Vistula, across Germany, past Ausburg and Nuremberg and over the Brenner Pass to the city at the base of the Apennine Mountains.

"Nik! Nik!" his brother was full of jubilation as he stormed over towards him. Excitedly he whipped out of his chest pocket two small, sealed rolls. "Our titles, Nik! Our documentation!"

Without any understanding Nikolaus looked at Andrew, shook his head and said:

"Titles? I do not understand you! I am expecting no titles!"

After a brief glance at Dominicus Maria di Novara, he continued with a smile:

"Well, maybe, perhaps a single document that I have become Doctor of Astronomy."

With disappointment Andrew looked at his brother who had changed so much since he had last seen him. During the long, long journey he had thought so many times about this moment of reunion with his brother. Now everything was different from what he had dreamt. The joy left his face and almost helplessly he looked around the room and at the strange instruments.

"We have become Canons of Frauenburg, Nik! Here on these rolls Lucas Watzelrode has written our names and put his seal on them."

Hollow was this news as it resounded from the walls. Nikolaus stood by the table, petrified. He did not want to lift his hand to receive the document that his brother held out towards him.

"Why? Are you not happy about it, Nik? There are thousands who envy us, thousands who would give a fortune to exchange places with us. And you! You don't speak a single word, and your face looks as if you had just heard about the death of a beloved friend. Do, for heaven's sake, be happy, Nik!"

Slowly and with obvious pain Nikolaus grasped the roll, opened it and cast his eyes fleetingly over the writing and the seal. Then devoid of any interest, he flung it onto the table from where it rolled onto the floor.

"Canon and Astronomer!" he murmured tonelessly. With his toes he kicked the roll. "Canon and Astronomer. I am afraid that these will sound inharmoniously together, Andrew!"

Brother could not understand brother. But Dominicus Maria di Novara lifted his head with a sudden jerk at the words of his student. He knew that with the advent of astronomy a deep chasm had opened between science and the Church and as yet there was no bridge yet to connect the two. He felt the discord in the heart of his student who, premonition had told him, would one day be famous and also whose name would be mentioned among the greatest scholars of mankind. Solemnly he stood up, left his armchair and stepped towards the young canon gripping his hand: "Copernicus, Canon and Astronomer!"

Clear and reassuring sounded the words of the professor, and they helped to create confidence in the honored one. With thanks he pressed his teacher's hand. Suddenly he felt strong and overcome with hope and this he expressed in one single sentence:

"Astronomer and Canon!"

Dominicus Maria di Novara understood the deep meaning that was hidden within the exchange of the two words. In this moment of being honored Copernicus had made a resolve.

"Astronomer and Canon!" Andrew said, full of happiness. Of course he did not know the full meaning of these words.

"We must get the best wine from the cellar," the professor interrupted the silence, and laughingly continued:

"Astronomer and Canon! As if that were not reason enough to celebrate."

Happily he descended the steps into the cool cellar where the large barrels were stored. Throughout the night and into the early hours of the morning, Andrew talked with his brother about their hometown. For a while Italy's wondrous ways, the rich city of Bologna with its blossoming gardens at the foot of the Apennine Mountains receded into the distance. For the two young canons the stars in the sky shone brighter than ever over the city of Torun, and the rustling of the trees was transformed into the gurgling of the wide Vistula.

Nikolaus Copernicus spoke little about the honor that had been bestowed on him in the German student house where he lived. His fellow students, however, were justifiably surprised that he came more frequently to the lectures on jurisprudence. At the same time he used every free hour to walk to the house on the flat hill outside the city. In the silence of the night, under the silvery light of the stars, the work which he passionately loved matured.

Once again he leaned against the stone wall that surrounded the terrace and measured with simple instruments the movements of the stars. Suddenly he felt himself roughly taken by the shoulders; he turned around and saw in the twilight the excited face of his professor. The figure of the usually calm scholar seemed to be shaking as if by a hefty storm.

Dominicus Maria di Novara drew Copernicus into the study. The candle had nearly gone out. For a while he seemed lost in a colorful map as he used compass and setsquare, and then he hit the table with his fist so that even the floor vibrated. With excited, restless steps he walked up and down the room muttering words to himself, which no one could have understood. Nikolaus did not dare to ask anything, but he felt that this was another hour equal in importance to the one when he had discovered the theory of the unchanging phases of the Moon. Silently he stood by the candle and waited.

The professor wandered around the room for a long time. Sometimes, when he bumped into a chair or the wall, it was as though he were dizzy. His eyes were burning and glowing with a fire that almost created fear. Never before had Nikolaus seen his teacher so excited.

Suddenly Dominicus Maria di Novara turned towards his waiting friend:

"Can cities, villages and lands wander, Copernicus? Can they move? A different place tomorrow from where they are today?"

Overloud did these sentences spout forth and the last was almost like a scream. The questions came so much as a surprise for Copernicus that he could not answer right away. After a while he shook his head:

"Of course not! They stand where they have always stood."

"Well they have moved, Copernicus. Here!"

With a sudden movement he tore the map off the wall, placed it on the floor and knelt before it. Copernicus took the candle off the table and held it close by.

"What is the name of this country?"

"Spain."

"Read the name of this city!"

"Cadiz!"

"Ptolemy calculated its position. I have done the same."

"And?" asked Copernicus slowly, still not quite clear where all these questions would lead.

"I have found that it lies a full degree beyond what Ptolemy calculated!"

"Then Ptolemy made a mistake!"

"His calculation is correct!"

"Then the error lies with ... with ..."

He did not finish the sentence, because he had shied away from telling his teacher that he thought that he was the one in the wrong.

"Yes, say it. The mistake is ... mine, Dominicus Maria di Novara. You did want to say that didn't you?"

"Well, yes, that is it!" the answer came hesitatingly.

"And what if I can assure you that neither Ptolemy nor Dominicus Maria di Novara has made a mistake in calculations, what then, Copernicus? What then?"

The student had an inspiration, a cognition that he dared not pronounce; he was afraid.

"What then, tell me, speak? What then?"

"Then... the Earth ... is ... not in a state of rest. Then... the Earth... moves!"

"...the Earth moves...." echoed around the room.

The professor straightened himself from his bent position and knelt directly under the light. He looked up at Copernicus:

"I too have thought of this. But you, Canon, have been the first to speak the words. You are bold. It is dangerous, very dangerous to speak thus openly!"

"Professor, it must be the truth!"

"The truth is always dangerous, Copernicus!"

The night outside was calm, clear and still. Not a breath of wind whispered from the mountains, and in the garden the trees were dreaming peacefully into the silence. Again Dominicus Maria di Novara ran from door to window, and from window to door.

"Columbus, the Moon, Cadiz...!" He was talking to himself. And each of these words was like a ladder, which rung by rung moved him away from Ptolemy and towards the far distant goal.

"Copernicus?"

"Professor?"

"Tonight we have cast away the Earth from its throne. Where is the new king to whom we shall give the crown?"

The night passed hour by hour. Slowly the tops of the Apennine mountains began to glow and a pink sky rested over the land. It was early morning.

"The Sun!"

Reverently Copernicus breathed the words. He felt the warmth radiating from the golden ball, and with his mouth slightly opened he looked at the magic spreading over the trees and blossoms, and then to the face of his professor.

"The Sun?" repeated Dominicus di Novara thoughtfully. Then he walked with the young canon out onto the terrace. Slowly the valley awakened.

5

The End of the World

Numbly the people walked through the streets of Rome and entered the magnificent churches in order to pray. Taverns, where red wine habitually flowed freely, remained empty and deserted. Tired eyes in need of sleep could find no rest during the night. Men, women, elders and children were fixated by the sky, in fear of a disaster that had been predicted in the last weeks of the year 1500. The earth was going to split apart with fires emerging from the abyss. Palaces and huts, temples and cathedrals, villages and cities, man and beast, everything was going to become ruins and ashes.

Preachers calling for repentance appeared everywhere, they stood on streetcorners and jumped onto stone blocks in market places, they sat on windowsills dressed in cowls. Their large eyes glowed with an unnatural fever and shone from unhealthy, bony faces. With imploring gestures they stretched out their skinny fingers to the sky and called out:

"Repent! Repent! When the moon darkens, the word of the Holy Scriptures

will come to pass. The world will turn to rubble, and the Last Judgment will be upon you."

The tightly packed masses bowed their heads low as they listened to the terrible prophesies; amidst them Nikolaus Copernicus was unable to move. Full of compassion he looked at the people. All joy was gone from their faces, some eyes showed resignation while others were fearful. His anger grew steadily as he listened to the preacher who was using the people's ignorance to achieve his own ends. For awhile he stood there undecided. He needed to think about the words of the professor in Bologna who had said that the truth was dangerous. He hesitated, but only for a moment, all fear left him, and with difficulty he pushed himself through the tightly knit crowd. Then he jumped up onto a high stone block next to the preacher.

The man in the cowl was shocked when he noticed the figure suddenly appearing beside him, and his sermon dried up because he did not know what to say. Into this silence Nikolaus Copernicus spoke his joyous message with a voice full of confidence:

"Just go home, there's no need to be afraid! On the third night from today, November 6th, look up at the sky! The Earth will be between the Sun and the Moon. The shadow of our Earth will fall onto the Moon so that it will be eclipsed momentarily. This means that the Moon will look dark for a while. You will all be able to see for yourselves how the shadow moves, appearing and then disappearing again. The Moon will be dark and then bright as it was before. Heaven and Earth will be the same as they were yesterday and are today. The world will not come to an end!"

The people were breathless as they listened to his words. They nudged each other and wondered who he was.

"He must be a German. Look at the long robe and his hood."

"He spoke courageously. It is dangerous to speak in opposition to the preacher."

"If only we knew which one to believe!"

Into the quiet whispering of the masses, into the restlessness, came the shrill voice of the man in his rough cowl and this time it was with renewed vigor:

"Do not believe him! He lies! An evil spirit speaks through him. Repent! Repent! The end of the world is near." With a sudden movement the preacher turned and faced Copernicus who was still standing on the stone block. He was looking sadly at the many people whose faces were torn by doubt and uncertainty.

"Who are you? Have you the courage to tell us your name?"

Copernicus remained silent. He felt the danger approaching him. People became restive when they perceived how the young German wavered. The hope that had glimmered for a moment in so many faces began to wane. Triumphantly the preacher called out, pointing with his skinny arm to the figure standing next to him:

"He does not dare! He is afraid of his own lie!"

The word reached Copernicus like a thrashing, which made him shrink. Then he stretched himself upwards so that he was almost a head taller than the preacher and spoke:

"Lie? Fear? Well then, you shall all know who has dared to jump onto this stone block in order to pronounce the truth! I am Nikolaus Copernicus from Torun, Canon and Astronomer!"

For awhile he looked across the sea of faces, then he made his way through the crowd of excited people and disappeared into the seething mass. He heard his name being whispered by many. He also noticed that the former depressing silence had begun to change. There was a new hope in the air and a trust that brought joy. Once more the shrill voice of the preacher was heard:

73

"Do not believe him! I speak the truth! He is lying! Repent! Repent!"

But his words were lost in the murmurs of the crowd as it dissolved into the alleyways and streets. Deserted by all, the preacher stood alone on his block. Slowly, his hands that were still pointing to the sky sank down.

"Copernicus! " he muttered to himself and there was an undertone of danger in his abrasive voice.

Two nights and three days passed by. The streets of Rome, which had the reputation as being the center of the world, were deserted. In many houses a name was pronounced with awe. It spread new hope and allowed the sadness to recede. In the huts of the poor and in the palaces of the rich it was repeated. Old men and women already close to their graves spoke the name quietly to themselves, while young girls looking forward to a life full of wonder did the same. The name Copernicus even found its way into the chambers of the Vatican, where Pope Alexander VI listened thoughtfully to the story told to him by a haggard monk in a rough cowl.

"Nikolaus Copernicus, Canon and Astronomer from Torun!" The Pope repeated the sentence again and again to himself, even after the monk had been gone for some time.

Meanwhile the young student wandered during these days and nights through the magnificent city of Rome. When he came to the Coliseum he felt shaken by its enormity and stood for many hours before its circular structure. Its stones had been so firmly entrenched that even through hundreds of years of storms, wars and destruction its foundations remained intact. He went to Angel Fortress where he knew of secret, subterranean dungeons. On bridges by the waters of the River Tiber following its course, he daydreamed, experiencing once again the distant River Vistula. Everywhere he walked he met remnants of the old Roman Empire that had once embraced much of the world but was now sunk into oblivion. Only the mighty buildings were a reminder of a proud time when the names of the emperors could be read on pointed obelisks and triumphal arches: Nero and Augustus, Caesar and Trajan, Marcus Aurelius and Caracalla, as well as many others.

In the old libraries on Mount Aventine he studied the writings of scholars and philosophers of long ago, their bodies long since turned into dust. The spirit, however, does not die and so these names continued to outlive time.

"Cicero!" he read on one of the title pages, and hungry for knowledge he became absorbed in these sentences:

"The Earth moves with greatest speed around its own axis."

He thought of the hour with Dominicus Maria di Novara in Bologna, the Spanish city Cadiz, and the answer which he had given to the scientist during that night:

" ... then ... the Earth ... moves!"

Again he had come a step closer to solving one of his many questions. A person who had crossed the threshold a long time ago, Cicero, confirmed his own thoughts!

Slowly dusk settled over the city of Rome. The night of November 6th had arrived. All the portals of the churches were wide open. The high halls of the basilicas were almost unable to hold all the people streaming in. The sky, which arched over a sea of houses, was clear and cloudless. The moon and the stars shone with a clear light just as on many other nights.

In all the alleyways, streets, courtyards and central places people looked up into the sky. Fear showed on their faces; from their trembling lips could be heard stammering prayers, and their folded hands were trembling in secret fear. There was not a breath of air moving across the land, even the trees were still. One could hear only the resonating voices of the preachers:

"Repent! Atone for your sins! The night of the end of the world has arrived!"

Slowly a soft gray shadow approached the full moon and began its path over it, for a while it was steady and then rose higher until the pale, heavenly body was covered completely. The streets were cast into blackness. Houses, people and trees became indistinguishable. An eerie silence spread everywhere. The gloomy shouts of the preachers rang out, horrible and hollow.

"The night of the end of the world!" stammered many people. And they waited for the moment when the ground would open up, when fire would rise from the abyss and destroy everything.

"Copernicus!" whispered others, elsewhere in Rome and without emotion. Their faces at peace they looked at the darkened sky in which the stars were shining brightly.

Meanwhile the shadow spread fully over the moon, and the moon vanished as if into an untold distance drawn upwards by invisible spirits. Then the first traces of the silver moonlight peeked out once again, at first only a small sickle hardly visible to the naked eye. Houses, trees and people began to emerge from the shadow, gradually growing brighter and brighter. But there were no fires from which the light streamed forth, rather the light of the silvery, clear moon providing a comforting shine to all around.

The earth remained unshaken. No abyss appeared. Huts and palaces rested quietly in the night with the trees rustling as usual. The River Tiber continued calmly flowing under the bridges. The cupolas of the eternal city seemed engraved in silver in the illimitable sky. Royally and majestically, the moon continued in its course amidst the beauty of the stars.

People streamed forth from churches and houses, they stood in the streets as if cast in stone, no one could speak. Motionless they stared at the stars, as if they saw them for the first time. Suddenly the paralysis left them. For many days and nights they had lived in dread, due to the terrible predictions; now at last they were freed from fear. They were still alive! Yes, they lived! Their joy was overwhelming. People who had never met before jumped into the air and embraced each other; they laughed and wept at the same time. Songs began to rise, at first only a few here and there, then other voices joined in and the city of Rome became a harmonious expression of jubilation and laughter. They were alive. Yes, they were alive. The good moon up above in the sky! The good stars all around them!

While they were enjoying their happiness only a few people recalled the name that, during their distress, they had spoken and faltered over so often. Now they spoke it, slowly and solemnly almost like a prayer:

"Copernicus!"

Others could not remember the name. The danger of the frightful night had passed them by. They thought of nothing but life and enjoying every moment to the fullest.

During this night Nikolaus Copernicus leaned against the trunk of an olive tree that stood on one of the seven hills of Rome. He thought about the shadow of the earth which he had seen wandering across the moon. "The shadow of the Earth was a circle, and the shadow was the Earth!" he spoke to himself thoughtfully. His face, with its high forehead, shone in the silver light under the dark branches of the trees.

"So the Earth must be a sphere. A sphere!"

This revelation passed his lips quietly but he was absolutely sure and spoke with determination. The wind picked up his thoughts and blew them over the city and into the countryside.

"The Earth is a sphere!"

Voices and calls reached him; it was as if they were coming from afar to this lonely place. Did he hear his name? He leaned forward and listened to the sounds of the night but heard only a confusion of calls and songs weaving its way up the hill.

"Who will remember me anyway?" he thought. And his eyes looked again into the sky that had revealed this new secret to him. He had already suspected it; now it was a certainty:

"The Earth is a sphere!"

Occasionally, during the following weeks when Nikolaus walked through Rome, people stopped still when they saw him, turned and said to one another:

"Did you recognize him?"

"Was it not he who told us about the eclipse of the Moon?"

"What was his name?"

"I believe that his name is Copernicus, a Canon and astronomer from Torun."

Repeatedly he saw glimmers of joy in the faces of the people who spoke about him. This joy meant more to him than honor and fame.

℘   ℞   ♁

In all of Rome the splendid palace of Goritz von Luxemburg was known as a meeting place of poets and scholars of highest achievements who had travelled from all countries to this center of the world. Being invited here was acknowledged as a distinction of the highest order to which only a few had aspired. Nikolaus Copernicus stared with disbelief at the messenger who had just entered his room.

"Goritz von Luxemburg has sent me and requests your presence tonight in the palace of San Michele as a guest of his circle."

Nikolaus was undecided; should he consent or decline the invitation? But the possibility of meeting scholars from all over the world who were so much more knowledgeable than himself was so tempting that he simply could not refuse.

Far too slowly did the hours pass by until the evening arrived. He could find no patience or quietude for his work. He read books and then closed them again after a few pages. He wrote on paper, but after a few sentences placed the quill, unwillingly, back onto the table. It was far too early when he began to walk the path to San Michele.

Hidden in a large park, amidst ponds surrounded by ancient trees with heavy, widely spreading branches, lay the palace. At the entrance a servant asked the name of the young guest.

"Copernicus."

He nodded his head knowingly as if he had been waiting a long time for this visitor.

"Goritz von Luxemburg has already asked for you a few times!" Copernicus followed the servant who walked ahead across a wide pathway of white pebble stones shining in a silvery light amidst the green of cultivated lawns. Still he was unable to grasp the meaning of this invitation and his heart beat louder when he imagined that in a few minutes he would stand before the most hospitable man in all of Rome, the protector and patron of all the arts and sciences.

Wide marble steps led to the entrance hall, which was immersed in a sea of lights. Thick carpets made every step inaudible. Costly chandeliers with innumerable candles hung by golden cords from the richly decorated ceiling. The corridors through which the servant guided the guest seemed endless. Copernicus followed him through wide rooms in which he saw men and women sitting at tables. Their spirited faces revealed to him without any probing that these were faces of scholars and artists. He walked as if he were in a dream. Momentarily he closed his eyes, afraid that this was all a deception or a fantasy.

A mild, warm voice interrupted his thoughts:

"Welcome, Nikolaus Copernicus, Canon and Astronomer!"

Kind hands reached out to meet his, taking them in a strong handshake. Suddenly he became inwardly still, all apprehension had gone. He looked for words of gratitude, yet he stammered helplessly. The pride, which he had experienced at first, turned to shame, that he, a student, was received into this circle. Gently he withdrew his hand and shook his head:

"Please, let me go! I am only a student who has neither written an examination nor passed one. I am not qualified to be here. In this place the most learned men and most famous artists gather from all over the world."

Swiftly he began to turn around and move to the door when he was guided to an armchair by gentle pressure. He sank into the soft velvet cushions. With a kind smile Goritz von Luxemburg looked at Copernicus:

"You are a strange human being, Copernicus! Others try their utmost to be invited to my house, but you want to run away again. Did you say student? No, from Krakov and Bologna I have different reports, and my friends in Rome hear your name in all places, on every street. They even heard it in the rooms of the Vatican. The Pope pronounces it often to himself. Student, no! A new time rises and an old world dies. We need men who have the courage to admit the mistakes of the past and strive for a new truth, even if it is dangerous. I know that Nikolaus Copernicus has this courage. I also know that he has the ability to prove the new truth. This is the reason why he has to be a guest in my house. A student? Yes, and the youngest in this chosen circle, but not the least in wisdom and courage! Therefore, once more: welcome, Nikolaus Copernicus, Canon and Astronomer from Torun, to the house of Goritz von Luxemburg!"

A servant brought sparkling wine in tall and narrow goblets on a silver tray, and the tinkling of two glasses signaled a sincere, warm and lasting friendship between the student and the older man, whom everyone called Patriarch. To be received and accepted into his house meant more, to most, than a reception in the Vatican or the palace of the Emperor. From this hour on Nikolaus Copernicus felt no more pride, only a sense of renewed duty and a commitment to reveal to the world the truth about the path of the celestial bodies in the sky. His hope was to shed light on the dark secret.

For many weeks, there was almost not a single evening that passed by without his being a guest in the palace of San Michele. Soon the name of the young student was respected in the circle of scientists. In many discussions, they had been able to admire the profound knowledge of the astronomer from Torun, and they came to him with many a question to ponder and study.

It was on one of these evenings that Copernicus escaped down the wide staircase into the quiet garden to avoid the humid air of the splendid rooms with their thick carpets and heavy, silk curtains. Deeply he breathed in the pure air. Then, over to the meadows, like a foal he began to leap; he was enjoying life as never before. His life was wonderful and beautiful. His future looked secure. At a little pond he bent down and picked up a flat stone and cast it across the water. It skipped two, three times before it sank, forming ripples. The more skips the happier he became, and he laughed joyously to himself in realization of his own unspent vitality.

He had not noticed that between the high pines Goritz von Luxemburg had been standing for quite a while watching him with a smile. Only when he heard his name called out by the familiar voice did he feel shocked and ashamed by what he was doing.

"Copernicus, take this and read it!" called out the Patriarch, as he crossed the meadow towards the edge of the pond. In the folds of his gown he held a parchment roll and handed it to him.

"I looked all over the entire palace for you. Then I was told that someone had seen you in the park."

Copernicus took the roll, unfurled it and began to read. With his hand he rubbed his eyes—was he dreaming? Once more he glanced over it quickly, then without a word his arms sank. Blue sky spread over the park while camouflaged birds sang in the tree branches. Fountains gurgled, and colorful flowers glowed in the green of the wide park. Could he be hallucinating or was it true?

Silently Goritz von Luxemburg observed the young canon's shy confusion. He smiled, took his hand and slowly they returned to the palace across the meadows. On the marble steps which led to the entrance hall between the chandeliers, Copernicus suddenly stopped, grasped for the roll in the pocket of his gown and held it out to the Patriarch:

"No! I cannot do it! Before the Academy of the Sciences in Rome, I, aged just twenty-seven, am supposed to give a lecture on mathematics and astronomy? No, I cannot do this! What could I talk about anyway? I am still trying to find my own way in the darkness. How could I possibly bring light to others?"

Goritz von Luxemburg slid the roll back into the pocket of the Canon's robe:

"They do not want the whole light, Copernicus. God can only give light in its entirety, not man! You, however, are meant to open the door and allow people to comprehend the stars. I know you can do this. I have great trust in you, and I ask you to speak before the Academy!"

Copernicus wanted to answer. Before the imploring eyes, the pleading glance and the determined words of the Patriarch, all his own contradictions were silenced. His head hung low and he felt the blood run to his cheeks. He felt shame and pride.

"You still have one week. The palace tower, with a view over the entirety of Rome and its Seven Hills, is at your disposal. I have had a room set up for you. You will find everything that an astronomer needs: paper and maps, measuring instruments and setsquares. If you have a wish, if anything is missing, let me know. I will not disturb you for the entire week. But then the two of us, Goritz von Luxemburg and Nikolaus Copernicus, will go to the Academy!"

In a state of confusion the student remained standing half way up the stairs; the Patriarch had been gone for quite a while, and he was still there thinking. Only when a servant came up and spoke very quietly and with respect did he awake from his reverie. Dragging his tired feet he followed the winding stairs up into the tower. He found everything as promised. Smiling, he stroked the paper and the many instruments. Here it would be possible to concentrate and work effectively. For a long time he looked out the wide window, seeing below the city of Rome with its towers and cupolas. The soft lines of the Sabine Mountains could be seen above a deep blue sky. Copernicus lifted his arms wide, very wide, as if he wanted to embrace the world with all its wonders and secrets, as if to grasp the stars and take them from the burgeoning heights into his handrs.

Throughout the week Copernicus covered many pieces of paper with his writing, and during sleepless, dreamless nights his pen flew over the papers and filled them with long number columns and sentences. He had to end many a sentence with a question mark. When each morning he read with a clear mind what he had written, he crumpled up or tore into pieces most of the pages, the calculations, and all that he had researched and written seemed to him so incomplete and questionable. Everywhere he found holes in his world picture. More painfully than ever before, he realized there was a long road of research still before him.

The week passed by in a second. When Goritz von Luxemburg picked him up to take him, by coach drawn by six horses, to the Academy, he had no papers to take with him from which to read. With empty hands he stood there, overcome by a feeling of unparalleled weakness and loneliness.

It was a sun-filled afternoon and Rome shone in all its beauty. Joy of life was visible in the faces of all the people who strolled through the streets and across the market places. Copernicus did not see anything. Before his smarting bloodshot eyes, snd tired from many sleepless nights, he experienced a dark, gray haze. Everything drifted in uncertainty.

As he entered the high lecture hall of the Roman Academy, he felt innumerable eyes upon him. The walk to the speaker's desk felt like an eternity. Goritz von Luxemburg was walking by his side, when, as if to gain strength, Nikolaus inadvertently and just for an instant grasped the Patriarch's hand. He heard his name whispered up and down the rows, and he could not understand why all these people who filled the hall to the last corner had come to hear the lecture of a young man who had not yet proven himself by taking a single examination.

Goritz von Luxemburg felt the excitement and fear of the young Canon. He looked at him and nodded. Every line in his old, dignified face spoke of an unwavering trust in him. Copernicus knew that he could not allow himself to disappoint him. He sat in the first row while the Patriarch greeted all the guests, but he heard the words as if they were spoken from far away.

The speaker's desk was empty once more as Goritz von Luxemburg came back to the first row, took Copernicus by the hand to help him get up, and accompanied him to the front. Pounding applause pulsated through the hall at this silent gesture, and the walls seemed to vibrate.

In this unexpected, thunderous applause Copernicus staggered forward. His heart beat violently and his head roared as if in a tumultuous sea storm. He still had no idea as he walked from the first row to the speaker's desk how he was going to begin or how he would end his talk. It was as if everything he had prepared had blown away. All thoughts had disappeared from his memory. An uncanny void spread before him and he shuddered when he realized that he had to fill it with living content. His long robe rustled around his slim figure, many folds casting from his slightly, bent shoulders down to his heels.

More and more threatening the lectern loomed before him. His fingers clamped onto the dark brown wood searching to find something more onto which to hold. He stood for a good while before the expectant audience. He struggled for a beginning and secretly he prayed that the right words would be given to him. His eyes searched for those of Goritz von Luxemburg and rested on his face; it was directed towards him in complete sincerity and full of trust.

Hesitatingly and softly, almost too quietly, the first sentences passed his lips; the people who were sitting in the last rows had to crane their necks forward to hear him better. Then, as he turned his head and looked outside into the deep blue sky spreading over Rome, everything disappeared around him, the hall and the many faces looking at him. More sure and resolute became the tone of his voice and his heartbeat calmed. He began by describing his own life's path, from the cabin in the Vistula ship *Silesia* to the sundial on the cathedral tower in Leslau, the long nights on the terrace with Albert von Brudzewo, and the house in Bologna and its terrace from which he had observed the heavenly bodies. He spoke about his calculations of the moon and the strange wandering of the Spanish city Cadiz. He talked about the moon's eclipse on November 6th in the year 1500 and about the conclusions he had drawn from it.

Breathlessly the crowd in the Academy listened. The struggles of the twenty-seven-year old Canon and astronomer revealed to them the error of Ptolemy and his own striving to understand the movements of all the celestial bodies. More clearly than ever before they surmised the end of a teaching that had its origin in Ptolemy and the beginning of a new world. The last words sounded, loud and invincible to those in the farthest corner of the hall:

"This is my entire wisdom: the Earth is a sphere and does not stay still but moves in the immeasurable universe. I will not rest my entire life until the veil is lifted from these as yet unsolved mysteries. With all my strength I will serve the truth as long as I live. To liberate the truth for posterity is the aim of every science!"

Sunrays glowed in the hall and played on the face of the young astronomer. The people remained captive in their seats as if they wanted to hear more. There was not a sound. It was as if all hearts had stopped beating before the courageous picture which Copernicus had drawn and openly acknowledged. Only when Goritz von Luxemburg rose and came to the lectern and placed his hands on the shoulders of the Canon, did the spell which had mesmerized everyone become broken. People got up from their seats and stood silently in the hall in the light of the sun.

Together with the Patriarch, Nikolaus walked towards the exit. He saw faces lit up with gratitude. He also discovered faces which looked at him with rejection and coldness, and he became conscious of how dangerous his speech had been. He had, after all, dared to openly criticize the teaching of Ptolemy and describe a new world vision that was blasphemy to the Church.

Goritz von Luxemburg felt the fears and concerns that lived in the young scientist as they sat in the coach on their way through Rome towards San Michele.

"Worried?" he asked him thoughtfully.

Copernicus looked up to him and silently nodded his head. In the sky big, black clouds appeared from the sea and moved over the city; they hid the brilliance of the sun.

"Copernicus, the truth does not know fear! And the house of Goritz von Luxemburg is a fortress of truth."

There was much comfort in the words as they sounded above the rattling of the wheels. The clouds sailed on disappearing into the distant horizon. Down on the River Tiber long, small boats swayed to and fro. Happy songs could be heard from the quietly, streaming waters.

Not long after, on a stormy autumn night, Goritz von Luzemburg felt his way up the steep winding steps to the tower room. Lightning flashed across the sky and revealed the pain engraved on the face of the Patriarch. Quietly he pressed down the handle of the door and stood for a while in silence before the bed on which Copernicus rested. Then he shook him gently by the shoulders:

"You need to get up, Copernicus!"

Nikolaus bolted upright, but it took him a while to regain full consciousness.

"What has happened? In the middle of the night?"

"Yes, in the middle of the night! I have received news from friends that your speech to the Academy caused alarm in the Vatican. It is dangerous for you to remain in Rome. Torun is quite a distance from here. Way up there in the land of the Vistula you will have more peace. You have to leave, Copernicus!"

The Canon stared into the face of the Patriarch; he could not believe what he had just heard. Thunder and lightning echoed from the Sabine Mountains. Leaves from the trees in the park whirled and scattered in profusion.

"Depart? Now, while it is night?"

"Tomorrow it could be too late. You must remain free in order to serve the truth!"

"What is the crime that I have committed that I have to creep away like a thief?" Copernicus remonstrated.

Goritz von Luxemburg quietly and without a word took the papers which lay on the table, placed them into the traveling bag, closed it carefully and gestured for the Canon to follow him. At the gate of the park stood a coach. Restlessly the horses stamped their hooves in the sand and reared up whenever the lightning flashed.

"My best horses and my most reliable driver will take you to Bologna. There you will receive further notice from me through Dominicus Maria di Novara."

Copernicus climbed onto the backseat of the coach. The strength and force with which the Patriarch spoke allowed no questions. As he shook his hand for the last time he was grateful that the dark of the stormy night hid his face. Only the shakiness of his voice showed his feelings when he spoke into the thunder.

"Thanks, thanks for everything."

He was unable to say anything else. Before his eyes, the rain blurred the figure of the Patriarch. It was as though the words he heard were coming from far away:

"The truth is always dangerous, Copernicus. I thank you, because you had the courage to reveal the truth, and I know for certain the day will come when we will be ashamed of the hour when in night and fog the Canon and Astronomer was driven away from the Timeless City."

The coach left with a mighty jolt and the horses galloped away. Everywhere it was dark; rain fell heavily and deep clouds hung in the sky.

"There are no more stars!" thought Copernicus.

In the palace from one of the high windows a light flared. As if lost, it shone in the darkness of the thunderous night.

6

THE HIDDEN BOOK

D rawn by strong horses the high, coach wagon stumbled clumsily over the wooden bridge, up the mountain and through the alley to the castle of the Bishop Low clouds drifted along a gray sky above the little town of Heilsberg. Its houses were almost lost among the myriad of dancing leaves, and a fresh wind swept from the mountains and thrummed the trunks of the trees.

Nikolaus Copernicus leaned out the window of the shaking coach and felt uncomfortably cold. Accustomed to Italy's mild sun and the deep blue sky of the south, he dreamed of silver palaces surrounded by a sea of flowers and blossoms. Throughout the long drive from Bologna to Padova and Ferrara, over the Brenner Pass, through Augsburg and Nuremberg and all the way to his former home, the image of his beloved Italian landscape filled his mind. Now, after all these many years, the familiar rough air of the north once again revived him. He could sense the salty smell of the sea in the air, yet longed for the sweet scent of Italy's gardens.

With a sudden jerk the coach stopped before the castle gate. The driver jumped quickly from his seat and pushed stones under the wheels to prevent the coach from rolling down the hill. Then he unfastened the heavy traveling baskets and carried them into the castle.

For a moment Nikolaus stood undecided before the horses that were winded and fighting for breath. He looked forlornly over the countryside spread out below him. Before he walked through the mighty portal he breathed deeply. It was as if he were afraid he would suffocate in the darkness that opened up before him. A two-story crosswalk was built on broad cornered, stone columns that lay in a square around the dark, inner court-yard; the massive, defense tower reached steeply above the red roof into the sky.

Shortly Nikolaus stood in a high hall with pointed arches and was announced to Bishop Watzelrode. Silently, unable to speak, he pressed the hand that welcomed him warmly. Deeply he bowed low, as was demanded by etiquette, to kiss the Bishop's ring with its magnificent stone. He took several scrolls from his leather traveling bag that hung on his shoulder and handed them to his uncle without speaking a word.

The Bishop bent over the parchments with considerable interest, unfolded one and read with the serious face for which he was known, for no one had ever seen Lucas Watzelrode laugh.

"Oh, this is your Doctrate diploma from the Faculty of Law in Ferrara." Copernicus looked out of the window where dark clouds were sailing across the sky.

"How was the examination, Nikolaus?"

"The professors from Ferrara were strict but just!" the question was answered in a cool and brief manner.

With an indistinguishable undertone the Bishop read that which was written in beautiful, Gothic handwriting on the parchment:

"The honorable and very learned Nikolaus Copernicus, Canon of Ermland, Scholastic of the Church and Holy Cross in Breslau, who has studied in Bologna and Padova, was graduated without any opposition and bestowed with a Doctorate in Church Law through the President and Administrator Georgius..."

He gently touched the sealed parchment as if it were a jewel and looked kindly and with satisfaction at the returned young man.

"And Medicine?" he asked further when he noticed that Nikolaus sat placidly next to him.

Copernicus gave the Bishop a second roll and again Watzelrode read:

"This official document guarantees and confirms that Nikolaus Copernicus attended the lectures on the Art of Medicine by the learned Girolamo Fracastro at the University of Padova. He was able to answer all questions satisfactorily and with a successful outcome before leaving."

Copernicus still stared into the clouds outside the high window.

"Well, then, you will be able to heal your old uncle very soon."

"Old?" asked the Canon shaking his head.

"Yes, old, Nikolaus! I don't live in an illusion. You see, when I let you go to Krakow and to Italy, you were seventeen years old. Today, at thirty-three you return home."

"It is only sixteen years, Uncle!"

"Sixteen years!" answered the Bishop bitterly and continued to speak: "Certainly for you the time passed by very quickly, too quickly. You lived in the beauty of Italy, and you cared little about your distant home. For me times were difficult, very difficult. The Turkish army came to the gates of Krakow, the Polish king, Kasimir IV, looked with envious eyes at our region of Ermland, and his successor, John Albrecht, was not much better. At the border to the east, Tiefsen, the Grandmaster of the Order of German Knights threatened Ermland with incorporation into his own provincial lands. These were sixteen heavy years and many a night I could not sleep. You have felt nothing of all this in Italy. Your thoughts were connected to the Sciences, Medicine and Church Law and—to astronomy!"

Lucas Watzelrode emphasized the last word. Copernicus contracted.

"You knew about this, Uncle?"

"A Watzelrode has connections everywhere. I knew and I remained silent in spite of it. I have been worried for you because your courage and striving for the truth has brought you into danger, a danger so great you cannot even surmise. It was good that I had close friends in the Vatican; otherwise you might not be sitting in Heilsberg Castle today, but in the dungeons of the sinister Engels Fortress! However, regardless of all this, I have been proud of you these past years, Nikolaus! Courage has always been one of the outstanding characteristics in the old line of the Watzelrode family, and it is because of this courage that they have become great and significant. With me it was courage in Politics, for you it is the subject of Secret Sciences!"

Suddenly the sky no longer seemed so gray to Copernicus, and the thick, stone columns were no longer so depressing and eerie. The strange and unexpected sentences spoken by the Bishop radiated warmth and hope, making him almost happy. Only now did he notice that his uncle's hair had become gray and thin and that deep wrinkles were engraved on his high forehead and around his mouth.

Nikolaus felt moved to express his gratitude for how he had been allowed to live for sixteen years in the light-filled world of scientific studies. He got up from his chair and as before bent over the forceful hand, which seemed to him rather more like the hand of a knight or a soldier than that of a priest, and with a protracted and sincere kiss pressed his lips to the Bishop's shining ring. For a short time he felt the blessed hands touching his shoulders and he quivered noticeably beneath this gesture.

It was on the highest floor of the strong, castle tower that Nikolaus requested to have his room and not in the lord's wing.

"It is unbearably cold up there in the winters and it is unseemly for a Canon to live where only the lesser guests are housed," his uncle tried to dissuade him.

"I have to be able to look up into the sky and see the Sun, Moon and stars, Bishop. Otherwise I cannot live!" declared Nikolaus willfully.

That same night he moved up into the castle tower where a room had been quickly readied for him.

Much to his regret Nikolaus was to have little time during the years in Heilsberg to spend undisturbed on his beloved subject astronomy. Lucas Watzelrode called upon him as a counselor and traveling companion, and many weeks during the year the Bishop was on the move. Ermland lay like a wedge between two enemy camps. During innumerable meetings and with astonishing skills the Bishop defended and tried to strengthen Ermland's independence and the freedom that were entrusted to him.

Often, the Bishop and the Canon were guests of the Polish king. Festive banquets and wild hunting events through the large, sprawling forests were arranged. They took turns in their attempts to solve difficult, political questions, and Copernicus, as Doctor of Church Law, had to summon his entire knowledge and search with cunning through the innumerable paragraphs of the law book to avert many a demand from the Poles.

They traveled to the place of the Grandmaster of the German Order of Knights and there too had to wage a fight around the green table to keep Ermland from being swallowed up. It was a dangerous game that Lucas Watzelrode dared to play: He pitted the Poles against the German knights and the German knights against the Poles, according to where he was staying as a guest and whenever the moment demanded it. In all his dealings the word "Ermland" always stood firmly at the center of his concerns.

There were only very few days and weeks in the year when the Bishop remained in Heilsberg and did not travel around the countryside. At these times Copernicus could dedicate himself to his beloved astronomy, and in these hours alone he felt fully human. Once again he used his setsquare and measuring instruments and sat bent over his calculations. The nights were spent with his papers and observations or absorbed in the writings of the ancient Greeks and Romans, in order to expand and prove his own theories of the universe and its moving, celestial bodies.

He looked over the many papers which he had taken out of the iron-clasped, traveling case. They were covered with secret sentences and numbers he had written in Krakow, Bologna, Rome, Padova and Ferrara, and over and over again he tested the calculations. The more he leafed through the papers, and the more he tested his own ideas against those of the ancient scientists from Rome and Greece, the more clear he bacame in his knowledge and the more determined in his resolve. Ever brighter shone the light which fell into the darkness of astronomy, and more visibly the many secrets of this heavenly science emerged. Once again his eyes hurt which reminded him of the time when he was working through the nights at the university. He overcame the tiredness of his body with tenacious strength. During these hours, high up in the castle tower, alone in his research, he was content and happy. Whenever Lucas Watzelrode decided to take another extended trip, only through immense strength of will was Copernicus able to once again leave his beloved astronomy and continue his appointed service. Even in the hour of leaving he was longing to return and continue with the work that had been interrupted. He wanted to forget the games of politics that were repugnant to him, and he approached his part in serving the Bishop as a counselor only with inner distaste.

Throughout the long weeks and months of these years in Heilsberg he persevered into the quiet nights with his studies of the early scientists. Finally Copernicus began to write down his own results from his copious calculations. Often his quill could not keep up with the speed of his racing thoughts; other times he would struggle with a single sentence for days. Page after page was filled with truths that would eventually uproot the belief of many centuries and revolutionize the worldview.

Fearfully he guarded the increasing volume of pages from the viewing of all who visited him in his room high above the ground. When he traveled with the Bishop across the country he hid his work in an iron chest with a triple lock or kept it in his traveling briefcase that he never let out of his hands. Not until the last sentence was written did he allow anyone to read these pages.

Lucas Watzelrode was the only one who, in an unguarded moment, discovered the anxiously protected secrets. On a clear, frosty winter's day he had climbed the steep winding stairs up to the tower room. In his hands he carried a sealed letter from Italy addressed to the Canon. Standing in the door he shouted loudly:

"A letter from Rome!"

Copernicus jumped up and eagerly tore the letter from the Bishop's hand.

"It is from Goritz von Luxemburg!" he said, with shining eyes. He stepped over to the window, broke the seal with the red crest and began to read. He forgot everything around him, the cold winter's day in the castle and the frosty storms over the countryside; he did not even think about his open book. The Bishop stood next to the table and saw measuring instruments, setsquares and open pages. Intently he bent over the uncovered pages; full of curiosity he cast a quick glance over the tightly spaced papers. With a quiet voice he whispered what he could only grasp with difficulty.

"All celestial bodies circle around the Sun, which stands in the center of all; therefore the center of the universe is in close proximity to the Sun."

His wide-open eyes were staring at the tiny lettering. He felt his hands begin to tremble and had to hold on to the edge of the table. For a while he stood there as if he had lost all his life forces, then he slowly stood up straight and went with weary movements towards the window. He stopped beside the Canon and looked at him for a long time. Deep sadness marked his face. Then he felt holy anger arise in him and he had to use all his self-discipline not to scream; his voice sounded quiet but there was an ominous undertone to it:

"A Canon dares to teach that not the Earth but the Sun is the center of the universe? A Canon ventures to affirm that the Earth is in motion?"

Copernicus awoke from his reading. Painfully he realized where he was: not in the warmth of sunny Italy, not in discussions with learned scholars. The thick, cold walls of the Heilsberg castle tower surrounded him, and a Bishop was standing next to him who resembled the hard preachers who had called for penitence in Rome. He had heard the question in his subconscious but now it was clear to him that Lukas Watzelrode had been reading his papers. But he did not shy away from the eyes that looked at him in such a hard and cold manner:

"A Canon? No, Bishop of Ermland. Science!"

"Does this mean that you place Science above the Church?"

Tauntingly the question was posed, but Copernicus answered quietly and unconcerned:

"The realm of the Church is belief, the realm of Science is all that which we research with our minds. The limits that have been drawn for both are as clear as the Sun, and everyone should leave these limits untouched and respected!"

For a while there was silence in the room. It was as if two worlds stood in opposition to one another, the Bishop standing for one, and the other represented in the Canon. Copernicus felt the depth of the abyss separating them. He immediately changed direction to a less volatile topic:

"Goritz von Luxemburg writes that Pope Julius II has laid the foundation stone for a new church of St. Peter in Rome. It is meant to become the most mighty and splendid basilica in the world. The most famous architects and master builders have committed themselves to this project, at the top well-known Michelangelo Buonarotti!"

Lucas Watzelrode did not feel any joy at this news:

"For twelve hundred years the old church had been in existence. Why should it suddenly no longer suffice?"

For a time he looked out of the window at the countryside, then jerkily he spun himself around to Nikolaus and in a loud voice, so loud that the whole room resounded and echoed, said:

"For over twelve hundred years Ptolemy's opinion was that the Earth is the center of the world and that everything circles around it. Why do you want to try and confuse people with your opinion?"

Copernicus felt the chasm that separated him from his uncle becoming more and more painful. Outside it had begun to snow big heavy flakes; a white, silver fog enveloped the landscape. Lost in thought he said to himself:

"Soon it will be a new spring!"

Lucas Watzelrode knew that these words did not only mean the spring in nature but that Copernicus thought of his new teachings. With a weary gesture he wiped his forehead; he still wanted to say something but turned silently and left the room with hasty steps. The door slammed shut more loudly than usual. Drained, the Bishop dragged his feet down the winding staircase and entered his gentleman's quarters in the castle. Copernicus was still dreaming into the falling snow outside:

"No one can stop the new discoveries, not Lucas Watzelrode and no Emperor, not even the Pope in the beautiful city of Rome, because the truth always creates its path, sooner or later!"

Then he took a quill into his hand and filled page after page with sentences, numbers and drawings. With even greater enthusiasm he sank into his work and into the book meant to encompass the new teaching of the movements of the heavenly bodies in the sky. On the table the pile of written pages grew ever higher. Before his restless spirit the picture of the firmament and its stars became ever more rounded and complete.

When the spring shattered the ice in the alley, when the first timid buds on the bare branches opened on the trees in the park of the castle, Copernicus wrote the final sentence to the last page of his voluminous tome. Breathing in deeply he laid the quill to the side, threw the window wide open and let the balmy air of March enter the room. In the red glimmer of the dawning day his figure stood high and slim against the sky becoming ever brighter. Only the title that he wanted to give to his work was missing; then his work, to which he had given his entire strength and for which he had missed so many nights of sleep, would be complete. He waited in the window until the glowing ball of the sun arose in the east, and then he spoke the strange words:

"The Earth rises!"

Then with careful writing he scrawled on the first empty page the very last word:

"COMMENTARIOLUS."

Once more he leafed through the pages that meant more to him than were his two hands filled with gold and silver. His lips moved quietly, but here and there his reading out loud reverberated loudly through the room:

"All celestial bodies have a center...

"The center of the Earth is not the center of the universe, but only the center of itself and of the Moon's orbit …

"All the celestial bodies revolve around the Sun that is situated in the middle of all; therefore the center of the universe is the Sun…

"That which we see as movement in the sky does not originate from a movement in the firmament, but from the movement of the Earth…

"Every day the Earth revolves around its own axis…

"That which we perceive as movement of the Sun is not a result of its own movement but rather the movement of the Earth…

The Earth has several movements…"

It was spring and the wind blew into the lonely room high up in the tower and carried his words far into the world. An era had come to an end, it stood at its grave, and a new one was being born. Copernicus looked at the calendar on the wall.

"1507! Spring, 1507!" he said.

The water from the melted snow rushed by and the fruitful earth was steaming, children found the first flowers and carried them with voices full of jubilation to their homes. There they looked at them transfixed as if they were the result of a miracle.

Years passed by. Lucas Watzelrode still drove far into the country and Copernicus accompanied him everywhere. He had placed the well-protected pages of his book *Commentariolus* into his traveling bag, which he never let out of his hands. At night he hid it under his pillow. The Bishop and the Canon traveled to Danzig and to Koenigsberg, to Petrikau and to the city of his youth, Torun.

They moved to Krakow, and while Lucas Watzelrode was invited to elegant dinners in houses of noblemen, Copernicus visited all the places of his long remembered past. In the interior of the university court, covered with ivy, he walked up and down under the archways and searched for the teachers he had known at that time. He found no one; they had either passed away or moved to foreign countries. He spent some time before John Haller's printing press shop and admired the crude beam with its heavy iron plates that imprinted the writing on to the paper.

The Master greeted the Canon humbly and showed him proudly the many prints that had been published by his workshop—bibles and calendars, writings of scientists and poets, maps and books of law.

"John Haller, can you also print mathematical drawings and books about Astronomy?"

"Everything, everything!" assured the Master and quickly added:
"Has the Canon perhaps written a book? John Haller can print it with greater love and care than any other printer could from Mainz to Nuremberg or indeed anywhere. And the name Nikolaus Copernicus would appear on the first page with the largest letters I can find in my printer's box!"

Copernicus heard these words and felt a daring temptation taking hold of him. With shaking hands he felt the papers rustling in his traveling bag and became aware of his *Commentariolus*. Already he felt his fingers moving to open the threefold zipper and he saw himself handing the work to the printer. Then in his ears he heard the same whistling sounds that he had experienced in the Academy in Rome when he was supposed to begin his lecture. From spirit depths he heard the voice of Albert von Brudzewo: "We have cast Ptolemy off the throne, but where is the new king?"

Suddenly he began to doubt whether the many pages in his traveling bag really contained the truth or whether perhaps there was one or the other mistake that had crept in without his noticing. With a sudden jerk he turned away and gained mastery over the temptation that was beckoning. He offered a quick farewell and hastily left Master John Haller's workshop.

"Not yet!" he whispered to himself. "Not yet! I will have to think everything through again. Much that I have been writing is only assumption. The proof is still missing. I shall begin a larger work and as soon as I get home I will begin anew. When that is completed John Haller can print it. But until then much time must still pass. And who knows whether a lifetime is too short to arrive at the desired goal?"

Never had Copernicus been so glad as when the horses pulled over the alley bridge into Heilsberg. Again he sat in his tower room for many days and nights. The sun heated up the high, red roof, storms whipped the walls, blossoms stretched up high and yellow leaves floated into the castle pond. New pages were filled with sentences, numbers and drawings as the great work of the astronomer grew steadily.

Commentariolus was hidden in the safest chest with the strongest locks, and when the old crumpled pages lay on his table the Canon always first carefully locked the door so that no unwelcome visitor would surprise him and learn of his secret before he had wrestled from himself a final and absolute certainty.

On one of these nights a messenger arrived before the Bishop's castle, his horse covered in sweat. He asked for the physician Nikolaus Copernicus:

"Lucas Watzelrode is about to die in Torun!"

On Sunday, March 28, 1512, when Nikolaus arrived at the Bishop's bedside, all the bells were ringing from the towers; he had come too late. In the high nave of St. John's Church the body of the deceased was placed among ivy and laurel. A few days later the Bishop began his last journey through Ermland, to which he had given his life's blood. Above the well-known streets and from houses in the many villages black flags flapped in the wind as Lucas Watzelrode for the last time entered his hometown, Frauenburg, the city by the turbulent Baltic Sea. Here he was to find his final resting place in the stone dome; he had led a full and busy life. In the spring sunlight the Bishop's mitre and crozier glowed golden above the heavy oak casket. Nikolaus Copernicus, his faithful adviser and companion, followed the slowly moving coach as it passed by the silver flowers recently sprung from the earth.

7

THE TOWER OF FRAUENBURG

Close to the Haffsea, at the estuary of the River Vistula were small and meager-looking huts with heavy nets stretched out wide from post to post. When the fishermen pulled up their wide boats and gathered up their red sails, usually late in the evening, the cathedral tower of St. Mary's, with its roof of shining tiles that stretched far into the darkening sky, was the only landmark visible. The mighty wall encircling the church with its corner towers was deep in darkness. The restless rushing of the waves alone disturbed the peaceful silence. Everyone in the little city of Frauenburg slept through the night awakening to a new day to resume their work.

Only in the northwestern tower did the light burn way into the night. The fishermen, who had to interrupt their sleep in order to look after their nets and boats, shook their heads and grumbled:

"Our new Canon, Nikolaus Copernicus, is surely a strange man. What can he be looking for when he gazes up at the stars each night?"

They shuffled over the sand between dune grass and silver thistles as they pulled and tightened their loosened ropes. They readjusted their anchors and quickly hastened back into their huts.

Lukas Watzelrode was dead, and the new Bishop of Ermland had found himself a new advisor and travel companion. When the little room in the northwestern tower became available, Copernicus rented it for 175 marks. He paid no attention to the sympathetic glances and scornful smiles of other Canons who found it strange that he would want to live in such poor quarters. What did they know about his need to live above the walls and rooftops? He had to be able to look into the sky at all times of the day or night, and nowhere was there a better place to be found than in this solid tower. From here he could daydream far into the distant fertile fields and out to the sea. The sky was visible in all directions except for the small section blocked by the cathedral's high tower.

Here he made himself at home, the quadrants were next to the wide window and on the wall over the table he hung all the many setsquares. Days and weeks, months and years passed by while the Canon worked incessantly on the task to which he had dedicated his life. Rarely did a guest find his way into the lonely tower and Copernicus hardly ever left his quarters. The work that lay before him seemed immense. His lifetime was surely too short to bring it to completion. The troubled times which raged in the outside world only touched his hermetic existence as from a far off distance.

Frequently the astronomer was seized by doubt as to whether one single human being could successfully and completely solve the manifold secrets of the sky. There were times when he was close to tearing the pages of the *Commentariolus* into pieces and burning them. This happened whenever he searched for proof and in the course of his research found mistakes and errors creeping into his calculations. On such nights he stormed out and, alone, walked along the beach letting his hair be ruffled by the wind and listening to the surging of the frothing waves. Once in awhile he could be seen loosening the rope from a stake and taking a boat. He would swing himself into it and row far out to sea, bobbing up and down like a nutshell on rising and falling waves. Heaven and earth became one and the silhouette of Frauenburg blurred before his eyes. Infinity surrounded him and there was nothing to hang on to. He would row until he was tired and at the crack of dawn he would let the waves power the boat back onto the beach. It was at this time that the fishermen came out of their huts to prepare for their daily trip. He observed them lift their nets into the boats and set the sails. He heard them crank up the anchor chains and watched as they pushed their boats out to sea.

Once an old retired fisherman stood by his side. He had become gray and jittery out there on the sea and was now only good for mending nets. Copernicus talked with him:

"You have been at sea for many years?"

"A whole life long!"

"Have you seen ships coming in from far away?"

"More than I can count!"

"As you looked out, what did you notice first?"

"The top of the mast, Canon."

"And then?"

"The rest of the mast, the deck, the hull, and then the whole boat."

"What did you think when you saw this?"

"I was curious if it was one of our boats."

"And when the ship passed and disappeared again?"

"For a long time I followed it with my eyes."

"For how long?"

"Until I could see nothing but the empty and lonely sea, and hear only the sound of the waves."

"How was it for you when the ship disappeared?"

"I believed that it sailed down a mountain after it had sailed up a mountain."

With a stick the Canon drew an arch into the sand, took a stone and drew the movement of the ship.

"What happens when I complete the arch?"

"A circle."

"And what is the meaning of the arch?"

"The Earth—land and sea, sea and land."

"Now draw your own conclusion. Which configuration is the Earth?"

"We have always been told that the Earth is a disc."

"Yet your own eyes and your own mouth teach you differently."

"Is it supposed to mean that the Earth is a sphere?"

Full of fear and nearly trembling, the old fisherman almost whispered the last sentence and felt as if he had committed a sin:

"Why do you ask me? You know it as well as I do. Yes, the Earth is a sphere."

For a long time the fisherman watched the Canon as he walked along the dunes.

"If one could only know what one is supposed to believe," he grumbled. Then he began to darn a large hole with strong yarn.

From this time on these strange ideas of Nikolaus Copernicus were shared in a whisper from hut to hut and whoever met the Canon glanced at him quickly and shyly, showing half admiration and half fear. The whole neighborhood knew that he understood how to read the stars and embrace secrets that gave one a frosty shiver when one dared to think of them.

There were other nights when the quill flew over the paper, scratching at times but filling sheet after sheet with new sentences, new numbers and new drawings. Again and again Copernicus opened the books of the old scientists from Italy, Egypt and Greece in order to compare his own observations with theirs. For weeks he sat looking at the Egyptian names of the months trying to decipher them.

"I must know whether 'Beuni' means February or October!" he murmured excitedly to himself. "All my further research depends on this!"

He had visited other Canons in their homes and posed questions but was met only with smiles and firmly closed lips which gave him no answers. He walked from hut to hut and asked the weathered seafarers for the meaning of the word "Beuni."

"But you have sailed to Egypt!"

"None of us learned their language!"

"Have you never heard the word 'Beuni' ?"

"We did not understand a single syllable of the gibberish which they spoke there!"

Discouraged he closed one door after another behind him. He grabbed stones from the beach and full of wrath tossed them far out into the sea.

He sent letters with speedy messengers to Krakow, Bologna and Rome; a few days later they returned. With shaking hands he opened the seals and, disappointed, let the papers fall or even tore them up into a thousand shreds and threw the pieces out of the window.

No one could give him the answer. Neither Albert von Brudzewo nor Dominicus Maria di Novara, nor Goritz von Luxemburg, nor Nikolaus Wodka. Despair overcame him and discouragement set in. Would he be able to complete his work successfully? One obstacle after another loomed over him and each one seemed to be more difficult to overcome than the last. Was his attempt perhaps arrogance? Was he trying to force his way into secrets that God did not want to reveal to a man of his limited intelligence?

For many nights the light was not extinguished in the tower room. Copernicus revisited again and again the part in the *Almagast* where Ptolemy describes the exact position of a star by the name of Mercury on the 30th Beuni of the year 486 according to the Egyptian calendar.

Then the trust in his own ability grew afresh and in painstaking work he began with the year 1515 and calculated backwards year by year until he arrived in 486. He hurried to the window, took the parallacticum, those strange three rulers with exactly 1414 dots, turned them around the axis and calculated through his own formulas the position of Mercury. In this way one number joined the other, one line followed the next and papers accumulated on the table. Often he was tempted to give up everything and to cast the mountain of paper into his fireplace. He imagined how it would crackle as it burned, but with unbending self-discipline he resisted the temptation and conquered his despondency and despair. He almost came to a point where he no longer knew whether spring had brought forth blossoms over the land or fall had yellowed the leaves, whether grain was already harvested or ready to be sown. He felt strongly that if he could just lift the veil off the secret word "Beuni," new insights would be revealed to him. Again the restless quill recorded sentences and numbers on page after page; his eyes hurt and his fingers trembled because he was so tired and weak. One candle after another burned down and dripped onto the table during these endless nights. Then finally he was certain and in a festive mood he wrote the letters of the final sentence:

"Beuni means the month of October!"

He stepped over to the window and breathed in the clear, cold night air deeply satisfied. He felt as though an invisible bridge were spanning a dark abyss across which he now could step, taking him into unheard of places. All pain and all past exertions were forgotten in the moment when he drew the final line under what had been a seemingly hopeless task. He lifted his arms and reached higher and ever higher as if he wanted to grasp the stars that appeared to be sketched into a clear, silvery-lit night sky. Taciturn and silent they followed their path, yet he was convinced that they were speaking to him. His firmly closed lips opened and he sang a jubilant song into the quiet of the night, into the rustlings of the lagoon, into the invisible drifting of the sand dunes and into the rocking of the boats by the rivers bank.

On a bright, winter's day the door of the attic room was opened and Fabian of Lossainen, the new Bishop of Ermland and successor to Lucas Watzelrode, stepped over the threshold. He was hot from a breathtaking journey.

"Copernicus, so here you are hiding from the people in this tower of yours!" he laughingly called out to the Canon.

"The Bishop, in person, coming to see me from Frauenburg?" Copernicus questioned and hastened to greet and kiss the ring on the Bishop's right hand.

"If the Pope and the Emperor want to honor Copernicus, why should not a Bishop do the same?" Fabian of Lossainen answered and winked good-naturedly.

For a while Copernicus stood there, he was speechless and totally perplexed.

"The Emperor? The Pope?" he spoke slowly in an unbelieving way. "The Emperor hardly knows my name, and years ago I fled Rome from the Pope in darkness and fog!" He completed the sentence slowly as if considering his memories.

The Bishop sat down at the table and pulled out two rolls from his fur-lined coat.

"Look at the seals!"

Hesitatingly Copernicus took the rolls and saw one seal with the eagle and one with the symbol of the Pope's crown.

"Do you believe me now?" asked Fabian laughingly.

"Take them back with you unopened! I am a man who has dedicated his life to the sciences. Politics and war, fights between countries, and indeed all power struggles are distasteful to me. I want nothing to do with them!" He handed the rolls back to Fabian, but the other only pressed them more firmly into his hands.

"How do you know that either one wants to burden you with political matters?"

"What else would a Pope and an Emperor want from a Canon who has studied law in Italy? They would hardly ask an astronomer for advice, because as an astronomer I am known to them as a heretic; I teach and believe differently from Emperors and Popes!"

He stepped over to the window and looked into the snow-covered country. One could hear the ice cracking from the beach. The wind swirled up through the snow making it look like a silver flag.

Softly Fabian von Lossainen spoke into the silence:

"In Rome, in the palace of the Lateran, important scientists and cardinals have come together from many different countries. They are deeply concerned and grieved. Our years and times no longer coincide with the sun. Festivals have moved, and the calendar is in disorder. Pope Leo X has asked that the year be calculated in a new way, that its length is decided upon, and the calendar rectified."

"What have I got to do with it?" asked Copernicus, looking out over the lagoon.

"It is known that you calculate the movements of the stars. As the course of the stars evolve so too does time change. You are the one who is supposed to calculate time!"

"There are enough scientists in Italy and France and in other places. They are not heretics like me. Who mentioned to the Pope that I should be the one to solve the problem?"

"Since the days of Alexander VI your name has never been forgotten in Rome. It is a great honor for you, Copernicus!"

"Honor? I do not know the word, Bishop!"

"The Emperor Maximilian is requesting your opinion!"

"I do not have any proof yet for an opinion!"

"You have time to research the problem!"

"By when do the Emperor and the Pope need my answer?"

"You have a long time, Copernicus! Three months, perhaps half a year!"

With an abrupt jerk Copernicus turned and walked slowly over to his guest, his steps heavy and measured. Stopping very closely in front of him he stared hard at the Bishop. The eyes looking at him were aglow with an inner fire so intense that the Bishop had to lower his head.

"Three months? Half a year? And you call this enough time? Go and write to the Emperor, write to the Pope, that since Ptolemy more than twelve hundred years have passed by. Twelve hundred years were necessary to move step by step to a new world cognition. I am not sure enough yet, Bishop! If the Pope and the Emperor can be patient for ten or twenty years, perhaps by then I can solve the problem. Perhaps at the end of my life I will know the exact length of a year!"

Fabian von Lossainen stood up from his chair so fast that the chair fell over backwards with a loud noise. He grabbed the Canon by his shoulders, shook him, and pleaded with him:

"I have given my word to both. Emperor and Pope are relying on you! You cannot leave me to deal with this alone! My word will not be turned into a lie!"

"Truth cannot be forced from science! You know that as well as I do, Fabian von Lossainen, because you studied in Italy with me. Everything has to grow and mature. In nature we know exactly how long it takes until the corn matures so that it can be cut and harvested, and we also know when apples can be picked and when new seeds have to be planted in the fields. But science cannot be calculated! It may be that I can give you my answer in one week; on the other hand years may have to pass!"

The Bishop breathed a sigh of relief as though a burden had fallen from his shoulders.

"So you agree to help, Copernicus? Can I write and give assurances to the Pope and the Emperor that you are willing to take part in the corrections to the calendar? That you are going to calculate the right length of a year?"

"Write what I have already said: Science is incalculable and will not be coerced. My entire life has been dedicated to the calculation of time and the movement of the stars. May God give me the time which I need to bring it to a successful conclusion!"

Fabian von Lossainen pressed the Canon's hand gratefully. He bent over the papers and drawings that lay on the table and, full of admiration, shook his head:

"There is no science which is closer to God than Astronomy." He took the measuring instruments into his hand and pointed them towards the shining sun. Blinded he closed his eyes and asked:

"With these simple angles of wood, you measure the course of the stars?"

Without saying a word Copernicus nodded. His thoughts were already occupied with the new task that had been given to him. He spoke to himself pensively:

"One has to know the center of the universe to calculate the time and only then would there cease to be a problem!"

Fabian von Lossainen became attentive:

"You are searching for the center of the universe, Canon? Since Ptolemy it has been known without a doubt everything circles around the Earth!"

Copernicus shook his head:

"Why then is time no longer aligned? Why do we have to correct our calendars? Why do we have to calculate the festivals anew? Why have the Emperor and the Pope called on me to research the length of the year if Ptolemy had not erred?"

"So, let me into your secret. What is your thinking, Copernicus?"

"Everything rotates around the Sun!"

The Bishop looked at Copernicus, his eyes wide open in consternation.

"Everything rotates around the Sun? That is blasphemous! This sentence is heretical! Do not speak it again!"

"At this point it is only an assumption, I struggle day after day and night after night with the final proof. If you see me as a heretic because I struggle to clear up errors and try help truth reach light, then tell the Emperor Maximilian and Pope Leo that the Astronomer and Canon from Frauenburg has dared to tear up their messages!"

With a fast movement Copernicus grasped the two rolls on the table and tore them in half. Slowly and clumsily the pieces fell to the floor. The wind blew into the room and picked up the parts scattering them into different corners of the room.

With no farewell, Fabian von Lossainen left the room. With a bang the door fell into its lock. Copernicus listened to the footsteps until they faded away. He heard the rattle of coach wheels drawn by six horses going around the cathedral and into the direction of Heilsberg. Heavy snowflakes fell from the sky. Heavy clouds hid the sun.

Quietly he picked up the pieces from the floor and threw them into the fire of the little stove, and the flames flared up for a moment. Pensively he looked into the glow of the fire and thought:

"All lies burn, clouds will sail onwards, and the Sun will once again shine throughout the countryside!"

He closed the window, sat down at the table and began to calculate the length of the year. Incessantly and without stopping the sand of the clock ran from the upper funnel into the lower. The candle burned strongly and sent its shimmering rays out of the upper tower and over the land. Fishermen in their huts saw the light and seafarers in their boats sailed towards the riverbanks guided by the golden light. They all thought of the Canon and spoke to one another:

"Copernicus looks up into the sky. But today the stars are hidden behind heavy clouds!"

8

THE MASTER OF ALLENSTEIN

L
ike a dark red mound the citadel of Allensteinreached into the sky above the lowly huts of the small town. Restless times were welling up everywhere in the region. Messengers galloped from all directions up the hill to the castle asking for an audience with the Lord of Allenstein, Nikolaus Copernicus.

They came asking for help and to receive protection against raids and surprise attacks from the Knights' Charter. In the long corridors of the fortress farmers and nobility, judges and peasants, men and women crowded at the door of his reception room in order to bring him their concerns and to hear his solutions. From early dawn until late at night there was a constant coming and going through the wide castle gate, one wagon after another rattled by without interruption.

With an aching heart Copernicus had exchanged his quiet room in the tower for the Allenstein castle. He had not felt any pleasure when he heard that the other Canons had elected him as Governor of the region of Allenstein for a four-year term. For a long time he had hesitated and rejected the nomination; unlike his good uncle, Lukas Watzelrode, his heart was not interested in honor or fame. In the end he succumbed to the constant pressure from the other Canons, and the new Bishop Fabian of Lossainen.

When long after sunset the seemingly endless line of visitors had ceased, and the creaking castle gate was closed, Copernicus sat over his books late into the night. They were not books about the Sun, the Moon and the stars, nor about the movements of heavenly bodies but, rather, about decisions handed down by judges that had to be scrutinized, church books which had to be evaluated and corrected, and there were petitions by farmers and settlers to be arbitrated. The quiet scholar had turned into a public figure who held in his hand the fate and well being of many people.

His own papers that showed the course of the planets, his descriptions and calculations on which he had worked for so many years remained locked up in his chest for many weeks and months. In spite of an incredible yearning he found no time to add new lines to the old sentences and bring his work closer to completion. Being the Governor of Allenstein demanded all his strength and time from morning till late at night.

Sometimes when he looked at the sky in the middle of the night, the light of the stars was overshadowed by a reflection of burning villages, he heard the tedious beating of drums and saw corn warehouses in flames; houses were burned down as the army of Knights moved ever deeper into Ermland leaving destruction in its path. With the greatest concern Copernicus saw the fires coming ever closer and he realized how the pain and horror of war threatened Allenstein.

One day he received a command from Bishop Fabian to prepare the city and castle for hostilities. In the middle of the night men were called to defend the city, gates were barricaded, and cannons were positioned. Pitch, brimstone and boiling water filled high kettles to the brim, ready day and night to be poured onto assailants should they attempt to scale the walls. Cattle and grain were brought into the city from surrounding villages. The large storerooms in the cellars of the castle were packed to their stone ceilings.

Copernicus appeared everywhere praising and rebuking, admonishing and encouraging. He alerted the guard who had fallen asleep while on duty, reminding him of his responsibilities; he allowed the farmer who had requested leave to go to his home village because his wife was unwell. When he was making his rounds he ate the same food as the men to whom he gave orders. Those who had to ready the cannons found him checking the powder they were using and measuring the angles of the barrels. In the castle's storage areas he calculated how long the stocked food supplies would last in case of a siege. He visited the sick and sat by their bedside, took pulses and heartbeat, bandaged wounds and other injuries, prescribed pills and strengthening juices.

The name Nikolaus Copernicus became for all men and women a symbol of justice and unending concern for the well-being of his subjects. When they talked about him they referred to him as:

"Our Nikolaus Copernicus!" because they saw that he was selfless and ready to share with them all their sufferings and joys.

The warring Knights' onslaught could not conquer the powerful walls of Allenstein. The stubborn resistance of the castle caused many bloodied heads for the enemy. After several anxious and difficult weeks the army gave up the siege of the city and withdrew beyond the borders of Ermland into their own province of Koenigsberg. A trail of burning villages and destroyed fields were their legacy.

Slowly the city returned to normal. Fires no longer smoked and church bells no longer sounded the alarm for war but announced peaceful evenings. Still Ermland bled from many wounds. Burned grain elevators had to be replaced, settlers had to be called onto lands where farmers had died in order to care for the farm-houses and land. Cattle that had run away needed herding; agricultural tools had to be handed out so that fields could be seeded to avert impending famine. During these difficult postwar weeks Nikolaus was constantly on the road. He traveled from village to village and from settlement to settlement to relieve pain and help the needy wherever he could. He used all his strength and the fullest extent of his knowledge. One scorching hot summer's day his coach halted before a stately farmhouse that had not been damaged. Its white walls glittered like silver in the sun:

"Farmer!" he called, and his voice echoed through the sultry heat. It was so hot the air shimmered. A broad-shouldered man came out of the door and recognized the Governor.

"Master?" he said and bowed humbly.

"Show me your best field!"

He commanded the farmer to enter the coach and follow his instructions. In the field that the farmer had chosen he tested the grain, checked the ears of the corn on the stalks, and scraped together some earth and ground it between his fingers in an evaluating way.

"How many hundredweights will you harvest?" he asked and stroked the waving stalks with his hand.

"About fifty double hundredweight, Sir!"

"Where are the borders of your field?"

The farmer described a wide arch from the pathway, along a small creek to some distant trees. Copernicus's eyes flickered as though he were calculating with his mind using the indications the farmer had given him.

"You can easily increase your harvest by another five hundredweight. The earth is heavy and oily and the field stretches further than I thought. How was the winter?"

"When sharp frost began there was already high snow on the seeds. "

"And the summer?"

"One could not have imagined a better one. Sun and rain came at the right time. There was neither hail nor storms."

"All the worse for you, farmer! I will ask five hundredweight more from you for the coming year."

"That is a harsh command, Sir! I did what I could and don't know whether I can manage to increase the harvest by this amount!"

"Come. On our way home we will talk about it!"

Painstakingly the field horses pulled the heavy coach through the soft, deep sand. A dense cloud of dust appeared behind the wheels and whirled into the air and did not disperse for a long time. The Canon spoke to the farmer about how to sow properly and how to fertilize, he spoke about the careful pulling of weeds and about the protection from rodents. He spoke to him as if he were speaking to a scientist about astronomy. The farmer was surprised that the governor knew so much about farming and wondered whether he had grown up on a farm.

When the wagon stopped again before the clean farmhouse, Copernicus asked the scribe, who sat in the back of the coach accompanying him on all his trips, to make a note of the increase of five hundredweight. The farmer no longer objected but bowed deeply and stepped towards the door. He stood on the threshold and waited until the coach had completely disappeared from view.

The Canon looked out of the window and examined the fields and the trees marked for felling; he saw how formerly burned houses had been restructured and now had new rooftops. He enjoyed the peace that had once again become a reality in Ermland.

When they came to a wide-open area without houses or fields, the driver was asked to stop and Copernicus left the coach. Quickly the scribe followed him.

"This is excellent soil. Why has it not been cultivated?" Irritation was in his voice.

The scribe leafed through his large notebook:

"The land belongs to the community of Schoenbruch, Sir. They complain about a lack of settlers to farm the land."

"Please note in your book: Nikolaus Copernicus's two servants, Albert and Hieronymus, will be settling on the land Schoenbruch each with three acres of land!"

The scribe hesitated; he was undecided as he looked at the Governor.

"Have you made a note of it?"

"Not yet, Sir …but … Sir, you cannot. Your two servants …"

With a quick gesture Copernicus cut any further discussion and said firmly:

"Bread is more important for the people than a servant for the master! In one week I want you to tell me that the servants have become settlers!"

Quickly the scribe's pen flew over the paper in order to mark the Governor's wishes, against which there was no opposition.

The coach rolled on over the wide land. They passed by dark forests and black lakes, waving grain fields and quiet meadows as well as some single huts that looked as if they were lost in the landscape. They came to an area of beautiful heather; the sun glowed in the sky:

"To whom does this heather belong?"

"Sir, it belongs to the community of Voytsdorf."

"We will go there right now!"

After a bumpy ride they came to some low huts over-shadowed by a very pointed church steeple.

"Take me to the Mayor! What is his name?"

The scribe leafed through his rough looking pages:

"Urban Alde!"

The horses stopped, stamping and snorting before a straw covered house next to the church. Water splashed quietly into a wooden trough on this beautiful summer's afternoon.

"Urban Alde!"

From the coach window the Governor stretched his hand out to a small, stocky man who came running across the street.

"Are you Urban Alde?"

"Yes Sir, the Steward of Voytsdorf."

"You need to be careful. The road into your village is very bad. The farmers need to bring gravel, the holes need to be filled and the foundation of the street has to be renewed! The wagons are sinking too deeply into the sand."

"Yes, Sir! When the harvest has been brought in it will be done!"

"The heather out there belongs to your community?"

"Yes."

"It must be cultivated to yield bread!"

"How is this possible?"

"First you measure the area: a thousand steps long and a thousand steps wide. Then you will dig fire ditches all around. The heather must be burned and the ground fertilized with its ashes and that yields the best field. In late fall you must plough and sow buckwheat. In the next year do the same, another thousand steps long and a thousand steps wide. In four years there will be no heather left, only an infinite sea of waving grainfields, and you will have plenty of wheat and rye in your storage places. If you need my help let me know in good time. Do you still have a question to ask me?"

"Yes, Sir! See over there, across the square in the little, slanted hut lives the old Streuber woman. Her husband has been imprisoned and now there is nobody to look after the harvest and the animals. The grain will rot on the stalks unless she is sent a worker who can look after everything. In the village we have too few settlers and everyone has enough worries working his own land. No one is able to help."

"In prison? What crime has he committed?"

"He built traps and caught wild animals."

"Was this his first offense?"

"Yes."

"How did he look after his fields?"

"I have no complaints against him, Sir!"

Copernicus turned to the scribe:

"Give me paper and pen!" He wrote a few lines on the paper and gave it to Urban Alde:

"Go to the judge who gave the verdict to the village and give him this piece of paper. I would like to pardon Streuber!"

"Thank you, thank you a thousand times, Sir!"

"Please show me his house!"

"It is diagonally across the market place, left and next to the church!"

Copernicus immediately jumped out of the coach, ran past the fountain and disappeared through a low door into the decrepit hut. He could hear plates being stacked and the crying of children. He tried to find his way through the dark. Following the noises he found himself in a smoky room, which had very little light coming in from its only window. A woman whose face was hidden by a woolen cloth tried to fan the fire by blowing into the opening of a little wood stove. When she saw the Canon she jumped up in fear, wiped her hand on her apron and bowed reverently.

"How does your husband treat you?"

Copernicus saw how the eyes of the woman filled with tears and how her voice trembled when she gave the answer:
"We have always lived together in peace!"

"Why did he have to go to prison?"

"Master, our hunger has been terrible! My husband could no longer watch our child crying out for bread. We had nothing to give him because we had to give up everything. Too much was expected of us. That is why he went out into the forest at night and laid traps in order to bring a little meat onto the table. The forester caught him."

"What are your dues?"

"Of all the fruit that we harvest—ten double hundredweight. On top of that thirty shillings is our rent for the land."

"What is the land like in your fields?"

"It borders close to a pond. It never dries up and always remains boggy.

The shoulders of the woman heaved in anguish as tears rolled down her overworked, haggard face. The child in the cradle was still wailing as Copernicus bent over to look at him with the deepest concern.

"He is quite pale. You need to take him out into the sun!"

"Master, he is pale because he has had nothing to eat!"

"This year you will be asked to give only eight double hundredweight of each fruit you harvest. And your rent will be from now on twenty shillings. Is this acceptable to you?"

"If you had a wife and a child, Master …" The tears choked her voice and she could speak no further. Only one more thing could he hear:

"My husband…"

The woman fell on her knees before him and kissed his hand. Copernicus withdrew it quickly, took hold of her arm and lifted her up:

"You must not kneel before me! But I will prove to you that I honor compassion above justice. Your husband will soon be returned to you. Urban Alde has already received my command!"

For a long time the woman looked out of the murky window and followed the Governor with her eyes. She folded her hands and repeated over and over again:

"God, please protect him! God, please protect him!"

Her pale worn face showed momentary happiness.

"Scribe! Make notes! The farmer Streuber will only have to deliver eight double hundredweight and he will in future pay only twenty shillings instead of thirty for his land!" called Copernicus in a loud voice as he approached the coach from the square and youthfully jumped. The horses pulled on their harnesses and with a mighty jolt they were off with dust whirling from beneath the wheels.

"The street is truly in a bad state!" thought Urban Alde, holding the note of pardon in his hand, and then he disappeared into his house.

It was late in the night when the Governor arrived back at Allenstein Castle. The doorkeeper left his room and walked over to the window:

"Sir, in the lane by the marketplace, Paul Sonnwalt's child is dying. The mother has already come four times looking for you!"

"Go and get my medical bag from the study! No one will be able to say that the Governor would let a very sick child die!"

Copernicus asked that the coach be turned around and drove into the lane; he knew where the poor family lived. He walked into the house and the room where a woman sat next to a wooden bed crying and a man stood staring silently into a corner. It seemed dark around him. He bent over the child, examined his pulse and listened to the heartbeat.

"Will he die, Sir?" the mother cried out in despair.

"It is a light infection of the lungs. Do you have a piece of paper?"

The man shuffled in a drawer until he found a torn piece of paper. In the dim candlelight Copernicus wrote a few words:

"Take this immediately to the apothecary and follow his instructions to the letter!"

Already he was standing to leave.

"Do you believe that my child will die?" the mother called again.

"In two weeks he will play again with the other children!"

Quietly he closed the door behind him. He was very tired as he climbed the steps to his study. Yet the weariness left him when he realized that he had been allowed to make a difference in so many people's lives, indeed had brought a measure of happiness to this busy day. It was this joy that gave him the strength to fulfill the difficult task of being Governor of Allenstein.

Weeks and months passed by. The war-torn landscapes and damaged villages appeared anew in all their beauty. Fields and forests showed signs of a well-ordered hand that allowed itself no rest but worked incessantly for the well-being of Ermland.

Only rarely, and for a very few hours, did Copernicus find the time to take out his papers on astronomy from the chest in order to continue the work he had started in Frauenburg. Then he measured with simple instruments the movement of the planets and examined once again the calculations from earlier years, always comparing and correcting. So the book grew page by page even in the busy days when he lived and worked in Allenstein. During the long trips through the countryside, he thought about his discoveries and reached many new conclusions. On clear winter nights when he sat wrapped in his warm, fur coat as the sleigh glided along the paths, his eyes were glued to the stars searching for answers to the mysterious wanderings of the heavenly bodies.

November 1517 saw early snowfalls. Deep clouds hung for days over the fields, and the walls of the castle were cold and frosty. Pensively Copernicus stood by the window. He looked out onto the countryside, but he did not heed it because there were so many questions on his mind and he was looking constantly for answers. Suddenly the door to his study was torn open and more excited than ever before, his scribe stormed into the room. His face was animated and in his right hand he held a piece of paper with large black letters printed on it.

"It has come with haste by courier from Wittenberg on the River Elbe!"

Quietly Copernicus took the paper out of his hand and read what he saw printed on the page. He read it again and then again.

"Dr. Martin Luther," he said slowly and almost solemnly. "Dr. Martin Luther! I will have to remember this name."

Restless, the scribe stood next to him, almost annoyed that he could not find the slightest sign of disturbance in the Canon. Finally unable to control himself any longer and with words stumbling over each other he said:

"And what do you say to the ninety-five sentences, that the Augustinian monk from Eisleben attached to the Castle's Church of Wittenberg?"

Copernicus was still silent and looked out onto the countryside. The clouds had separated leaving a small, silver lining that shone in the darkness. Slowly the Canon turned around, went to the table where papers and measuring tools lay, and took a leaf of paper that was half covered with writing.

"I believe that a new time is coming. Much has been done wrongly and much must be put right. Dr. Martin Luther! I will have to remember the name. He wants truth in the Church just as I research the truth in the stars! Somehow we belong together!"

"He is far too bold!" responded the scribe with indignation.

Copernicus answered firmly: "It is always daring to fight for the truth—and dangerous! For him perhaps even moreso than for me."

Then he laid the two papers— the news from Wittenberg and the page that he was working on—back onto the table and let the scribe know that his services were no longer needed. With a deep bow and walking backwards, the scribe left the room.

From this day onwards in November 1517, the Canon immersed himself ever more deeply into his work. Every hour he was free from his office tasks he spent studying ancient astronomers and calculating and observing the night sky. Papers piled up and line after line was written untiringly. The seasons passed by. Twice it was summer and twice winter. Twice the trees blossomed, and twice the autumn wind whirled the dying leaves away from their branches.

In 1519 the Governor went to the Bishop to account for his activities in Allenstein; he listened to the praises silently and calmly. Every honor he rejected with a few modest words: "I did only that which was my duty!"

Joy radiated from his face. But the other Canons believed that it was happiness because of the praises that had been bestowed on him for his loyal governorship; they were wrong. They knew nothing of his secret work during the quiet hours and of his book in which he wrote about the movement of the heavenly bodies.

After four long, hard years Copernicus returned once again to his beloved, homey room in the Frauenburg tower; he could have shouted for joy and gratitude. He pulled the armchair close to the window through which he saw the clear night sky and solemnly lit a candle. He opened the last page of the book, completed shortly before leaving Allenstein, and he read once more with a loud voice that which was written there in large letters:

"In the center of all the heavenly bodies reigns the Sun. Who would want to give to this heavenly light a different or better place, because from here she can send her light into the whole cosmos? So, indeed, does the Sun, sitting on her majestic throne, guide the circling family of the stars."

The sea surged onto the beach, and the shadows of the sailboats danced up and down on the waves. Copernicus listened into the night, and happy songs sounded to his ears from everywhere like a mighty chorus in a sleeping, peaceful world.

9

ELBING, ROSE MONDAY
BEFORE LENT

Ligh up on the walls of Frauenburg's Cathedral on the tower
pinnacles black flags flapped and waved in the wind. The
church bells were muffled as they
proclaimed far and wide into the countryside of Ermland the death of Bishop Fabian
von Lossainen. With bowed heads and
measured steps the canons walked
through the streets to the high refectory.
The assembly hall was decorated som-
berly. Over their silk robes the canons wore
thick, fur coats because the snow-covered
land in the winter of 1523 was in the icy
grip of bone-jangling coldness. Even now,
on this day of the funeral, a successor to
Fabian had to be chosen from their midst,
to govern Ermland until a new Bishop was
elected and confirmed by the Prussian and
Polish kings.

The refectory was completely covered with black velvet
cloth right up to the arched and pointed ceiling. Yellow candles
burned with a golden flicker along the stone columns. It smelled
of flowers and death and there was complete silence in the darkened room. Only when the canons entered through the heavy,
oaken door and moved to their accustomed places, could the rustling of their silken robes be heard like the swishing of a distant

wind or like the foaming of waves against the lagoon. On a large table covered in black, everyone had pen, ink and paper in front of him in order to write down the name of the man whom they deemed worthy to govern Ermland for the interim.

A very old man with long, white hair falling onto his shoulders got up from his place in the first row. He spoke quietly and with a trembling voice, yet his speech was clear and distinct and could be heard in the farthest corner of the refectory:

"Bishop Fabian von Lossainen is dead!"

The Canons got up from their high-backed, wooden armchairs, folded their hands and bowed their heads. Silently they remembered the dead Bishop. The candles burned undisturbed by any movement of air, and the large death bell tolled with slow, dark knells. It sounded until the sand filled both funnels of the clock exactly halfway, then the last toll faded away with a vibrating and shy tone.

The Canons reseated themselves comfortably; only the eldest remained standing and spoke to the silent, expectant group:

"In a secret vote the General Regent must be determined from our midst. Ermland's fate will rest in his hands until a new Bishop ascends to the dais of the cathedral!"

For a long time there was not a sound, then the rustling of papers could be heard and hands grasped for pen and ink in order to write down one name. When the speaker saw that all the papers lay folded on the table, he took the crosier of the past Bishop and collected them. With trembling hands he spread them out before him and began to place them into piles. His wilting lips whispered the names. The Canons were attentive and curious, leaning forward in their seats, waiting with baited breath and full of inner emotions for the final decision.

"The Cathedral Chapter of Frauenburg has elected Nikolaus Copernicus as the General Regent for Ermland!"

Loud and clear sounded the words through the hall. With a gesture of his hand the speaker requested one of the canons to come up and review the ballots.

"Nikolaus Copernicus!" the Canon repeated clearly and solemnly, then he walked back to his place. Both delighted and disappointed faces searched for the figure of the man who had been chosen by the majority to govern Ermland. He sat modestly and unobtrusively in the last row by the door, his head was lowered and he seemed to be motionless as he reclined in his chair. His hands tightly grasped the beautifully carved armrests. Slowly movement began to flow through his body. With difficulty he stood up as if he already felt the weight of the task that had been laid upon his shoulders. His large, open eyes searched for the quiet light of the yellow candles as he began to speak:

"The choice that you have made I experience as a sincere trust. This trust is a high honor that has been bestowed on me. In spite of this I ask you for one night for reflection. Tomorrow morning at first bell, the Chapter of Frauenburg will hear my decision!"

He was the first person to leave the veiled room; he crossed the courtyard in front of the cathedral and climbed up to his beloved room in the northwestern tower. The hard frost had conjured up ice flowers on his window and as the moon and stars encircled the sky, the crystals glimmered in countless, golden points. During this night Copernicus found neither the peace to sleep nor concentration for work. Restless he wandered to and fro, here and there; he blew into the fireplace to fan new flames. His hands were cold and he warmed them on the warm stone. The simple measuring instruments and the wooden angle hung untouched on the wall, pieces of paper blank and full were left carelessly on the table. His fingers could not pick up the quill to resume work. Without a sound the sand fell through the hourglass. The big, round candle burned lower and lower until it fizzled out and the wick lost its last glow. Only the flickering of the red fire hovered ghostlike through the room.

His footsteps sounded hollow on the wooden floor.

"If I were a Lukas Watzelrode I would accept their choice and the task with joy. But long ago my heart chose the stars, and there is still a large work to be completed!" Copernicus murmured to himself.

He leafed through the pages on which he had written his discoveries many years ago. He looked at a drawing that he had just put the final strokes to when the courier had entered the tower room to request his presence at the meeting:

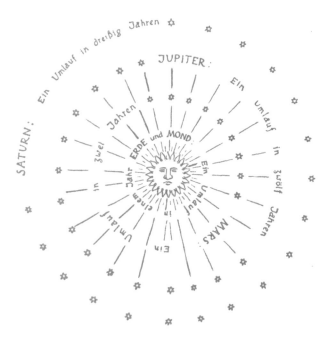

By the time he put the paper to one side and the world of stars took on an air of unreality, the early morning light was resting on the frozen windows. The stove was completely cold because the fire had burned out long ago. He realized that he was shivering. In spite of it he flung the window wide open. Far below lay the huts; their inhabitants were in the last throes of sleep. In dreamlike silence, the waters of the lagoon no longer surged against the bank but lay torpid under a thick layer of ice. He thought of the people in houses of the city and in the many different villages and hamlets in Ermland, from Frauenburg to Allenstein and from Braunsberg to Heilsberg. It was as if he experienced their worries and their needs more strongly than ever before, but also their hopes and their trust. Love for this land welled up in him, comforting yet demanding at the same time. Could he allow himself to value more highly his work with the stars than with people? Or could he delay again the calling that had come to him in the quietness of his study and take on that which would place him once more in the public eye? Before him rose the faces of all the people to whom he had given joy during his trips through Allenstein as Governor.

The light of the early morning sent its radiance from the sky to the rooftops, the streets and onto the snow-covered fields. It flooded the silent forests and calm sea. At that moment Nikolaus Copernicus knew that he was not allowed to live his life only for himself. With trembling fingers he fumbled for paper and pen to write down his decision. There was a reflection of joy and pain in his face, which revealed a rare beauty. He grasped for the little silver bell and rang; footsteps approached and he gave the folded piece of paper to the entering servant:

"Take this paper to the oldest Canon before the first bell!"

When the bell finally began to ring it sounded the name of Nikolaus Copernicus far into the awakening land. The General Regent of Ermland listened to its sounds, then he closed and locked up his work on astronomy and got ready to go to the cathedral in order to take the oath before the graves of the deceased bishops. There he would be entrusted with the insignia of power.

Once again, just like during the years when he was Governor of Allenstein, he traveled through Ermland and looked after order and justice. With tact and intelligence he smoothed over disagreements and defended Ermland's freedom against the Kings of Prussia and Poland as well as against the highest rank of the Order of the Knights. His special care, however, went to the poor, as he did everything in his power to alleviate their plight.

Only too often on his trips he heard bitter complaints that the price of bread was too high. He met hungry children with sunken cheeks and dull eyes in which there was not a glimmer of light. The urgent need moved him to tears and for a long time he thought about how he could best regulate the price of bread. He looked at the different kinds of grains and examined meticulously how much bread could be baked with every bushel. He made surprise visits to bakeries and examined the books of the bakers. He calculated the sums spent on salt, sourdough, heating and transport. In long nights he worked with all the information collected from his many trips and then he was ready to proclaim a new law that was taken to all cities and villages by special messengers and hung on notice boards.

The poor people read the words that put an end to profiteers and inflated prices. They read the name of the General Regent who had made the law effective by his seal and signature. The name Nikolaus Copernicus inspired confidence and trust in them, a consoling light in their heavy plight.

The snow crunched loudly when the Canon returned late at night across the churchyard to his tower room. He did not want to miss that, even as General Regent. The moon stood full and round in the sky and the alleys and houses of the sleeping city seemed transformed into fairy tale land. For a while Nikolaus breathed deeply, lost in the surrounding peace and quiet, then he climbed slowly the steep steps of the tower, opened the door, and stepped into his room.

Out of the half darkened room a figure came towards him:

"Nik, finally!"

Copernicus recognized his childhood friend from Torun:

"Tiedemann!" he called out, full of surprise, and lit a candle on the embers in the stove. Then he grabbed his friend by the shoulders and held the candle to his face.

"Tiedemann!" he repeated once more, placed the candle on the table and ran into the cellar. Out of breath he returned with two glasses and a bottle in his hands. Golden sparkling wine—the glasses clinked with a silvery tone, then were emptied in a single drought.

"You look so serious, Tiedemann. Do you have worries that bring you to me?"

The guest shook his head, shifted his position awkwardly and drank one last little drop before he began:

"Do you remember the Portuguese named Ferdinand Magellan, Nik?"

"Magellan…Ferdinand Magellan?" Copernicus repeated and rubbed his eyes and forehead with his hands:

"Let me think, Tiedemann! The many tasks I carry as General Regent seem to confuse me considerably. There is nothing but strife and politics, misery and complaints all day long from morning to night. Let me think! Magellan … Ferdinand Magellan?"

He propped his head on his hands and elbows and stared into the flames of the flickering fire. Suddenly he sat up with a smile on his face, and in a lively way he said:
"Was he not the one who three years ago—it must have been 1519—tried to sail around the Earth?"

Tiedemann nodded:

"It is not too long ago that his crew returned home to Portugal."

"And Magellan himself?"

"He was murdered in the Philippines!"

"Do you know more? You must tell me everything, Tiedemann, even if it takes the whole night. It could be important for my calculations!"

"This is the reason why I came from Allenstein to you. A mystery is hidden behind this daring journey. If anyone can solve the problem, you are the only one who can do it!"

Copernicus rejected the praise of his friend with a swift gesture of his hand.

"A mystery?" he asked full of tension.

"The enthusiastic seafarers hardly dared to get off their boats. They are deeply disturbed."

"I don't understand. Did they not return to praise and honor?"

"In their ships logs, from the documents and drawings that were kept throughout the three years of traveling, one day is missing. It cannot be explained. And yet their records are accurate."

"A day is missing? A ... day ... is missing?"

Copernicus jumped up, pushed the half-filled glass aside, opened a wall cupboard and took out a large map, which had on it all the known countries on Earth for that time. Hastily he unrolled the scroll and spread it on the floor.

"Can you describe the route of the Portuguese? I have to hear this once more exactly."

"On the 10th of August, 1519, Magellan left from San Lucar, the harbor city at the mouth of the Guadalquivir, with five sailboats. Through good fortune he found the passage into the south sea and gave it the name Pacific Ocean, because on his trip he had only good weather. Shortly after he discovered the Philippines, he was slain with several of his companions. The others continued the journey and arrived, towards the end of 1522, in the harbor of San Lucar on the only ship left to them after sailing around Africa. This was the first journey around the world! Three years it took them!"

Copernicus bowed over the map tracing with charcoal the path of the brave seafarers. Silently he waited for Tiedemann to continue.

"And in spite of it there are still many who do not believe that the Earth is a sphere. They say on the lower half the people would have to hang upside down. How could that be possible? Would not all people descend into hell in the underworld? They still talk about the legendary Paradise Mountain, which is supposed to reach up to the Moon-disc. Still today they believe that there are eagles that can carry elephants through the air, lions and serpents with several hundred heads, terrible spirits with six arms and with eyes on their breasts and claws as long as Turkish sabers. The mystery of the missing day has intensified the imagination of the people and made them even more superstitious and fearful. I have already sacrificed many nights to solve this secret. Finally I could not stand it any longer—I had to come to you. You have to solve the riddle. I am absolutely certain that you can do it, Nik!"

Copernicus was still following the journey of the Portuguese with his charcoal.

"They traveled west!" he spoke. "Always west they sailed!"

Excitedly he jumped up from the floor, ran up and down in his room, stepped up to the table, drew marks on an arch, and wrote numbers on a piece of paper. He went to Tiedemann, grabbed him by the shoulders and shook him with all the strength he had. His eyes were aglow and his ruffled hair fell over his high forehead.

"The Sun, the Sun!" he whispered in a hoarse voice. "Where does she seem to appear, Tiedemann?"

"In the east of course. Every child knows this. What does this question have to do with the secret of the missing day?"

"In the east, yes. And it seems that she sets in the west!"

Again he bent over the map with the large blue areas that signified the seas and the light areas for land. Once more he followed the same thoughts and the journey of the sailboats with the fearless men. Without a word he sat down at the table, drew the candle very close to the paper, took a set square and charcoal in hand and began to write and draw.

Paper after paper was covered with numbers and symbols. Here and there he crumpled a piece of paper with an unwilling movement and let it fall on the floor. He kicked it away with his foot as far out of his reach as possible. His lips constantly moved, but what he said was inaudible, just unclear mumbling. Once in a while he breathed so deeply that the candle flickered and threatened to die but then it would straighten up again and continue to burn with a sure flame.

He forgot everything around him: the wine, untouched next to him, his childhood friend Tiedemann, the map on the floor, the fire in the stove. He did not notice how the sand in the hourglass had long since run out. Time and the world seemed to be at a standstill. Only his fingers with the charcoal moved in a feverish rush over the pages, which lay disorganized on the table.

After a long while Copernicus lifted his head and spoke clearly and loudly:

"It must be dependent on the Sun and with the movement of the Earth around the Sun, Tiedemann! With the Sun, time always comes and goes!" He waited in vain for a response from his friend. When he looked around the room he saw his guest, overtired from his journey, lying stretched out on the simple camp bed, his regular breathing floating through the silence. Copernicus smiled. Then he stood up, pulled a cover from a chest and with a caring gesture laid it over Tiedemann's sleeping body.

"Sleep well, friend!" he spoke with a quiet smile. "You have not taken the Regent's resting place! He has no time to dream and sleep. The riddle of the missing day will not give him peace until it is solved. Good night, Tiedemann!"

On tiptoe he returned to the table and placed a tall book upright before the candle so that its shine would not bother his sleeping friend. Then he took the pencil once more into his hand and wrote, crossed out, began again and obliterated what he had written, calculated and thought for a long time.

Outside in the countryside the night traveled, increasing and then decreasing. Moon and stars followed their paths and the northwestern tower reached into the sky with clear and sharp contours.

When late in the morning Tiedemann awoke, he was alone in the astronomer's study high up in the tower. Confused, he looked around. He had first to recollect where he was. He felt ashamed that he had fallen asleep while his friend was calculating. He was annoyed with himself. He got up and walked over to the table. His glance fell on a piece of paper that bore his name. Curiously he took it in hand and read:

> Dear friend, Tiedemann!
> Business as General Regent has called me to Graudenz. You will not have time to wait until I return. Take the papers that lie rolled up on the table with you to Allenstein. I have calculated: he who travels west around the Earth will save a day. There is no mystery hidden in it. The cause lies in

the Sun together with the Earth's movement. Please bring these papers back or send them to me by courier when you have finished with them.

Nik.

A short while later Tiedemann was galloping on a rested and freshly bridled horse on the road towards Allenstein. His coat blew in the wind behind him and his hair fluttered in the January chill. In his leather bag was the roll from his friend with all the calculations. Determined, he guided his horse carefully by the pressure of his thighs, keeping it on track, and reached Allenstein more quickly to read the pages that solved the riddle which had set half the world in turmoil.

When the summer of this year ended and the fields were harvested, the new Bishop Mauritius Ferber, from a Danzig genealogy, moved with pomp and splendor into the Frauenburg castle. Hard and strict were his eyes in a haggard face, and the people felt fear when they met him. In the festively decorated throne room, Copernicus gave account of his administration, and his voice sounded happy and light because he thought of his work and interest in astronomy to which he would now be able to give all his strength and time. He felt freed from a pressing burden, and he walked more upright and breathed more deeply than he had in these previous months when he bore the honorable but weighty title of General Regent of Ermland.

Silently Mauritius Ferber heard the report. He found nothing that he could criticize concerning the Canon's administration. The books were in order and the financial picture looked extremely favorable. All the storage places were filled up to the roofs with grains; moreover, he had seen happy contented faces when he moved into Frauenburg. The quiet inquiries that he had made through some trusted friends were all full of praise and recognition for the activities of the General Regent.

The pursed lips of the new Bishop opened, and coldness lived in the words he spoke, so cold that Copernicus felt a shock. He was not looking for praise or recognition; what he had done was his duty. But the sound of the voice was harsher than he had expected:

"I have examined your administration, and I find nothing to criticize. Before I let you return to your previous duties of a Canon, I have to warn you to never, either in word or writing, work against the Church. I have heard strange things, Copernicus. I know that you understand more about the heavenly bodies than anyone else in this country, indeed, perhaps even in Europe. If, however, you teach that the Sun remains firm and the Earth moves, I will call it treason. I warn you, Nikolaus Copernicus!"

He lifted his hand and offered the ring for a kiss by the Canon, rang the bell, and asked the servant to lead Copernicus out of the room. Tall and haggard, the figure of the Bishop stood between the candles and flags and motionless he watched the departing Canon. After the door had fallen quietly into its lock, he pushed the curtain back and beckoned to a hidden, squatting figure:

"You know your task, Hosius?"

"To watch over the Canon and find out the content of his secret writings."

Noiselessly, the spy Hosius left the room. Quietly the curtain opened, and as he disappeared behind it the flags and candles flickered in the draft.

Copernicus was far too involved in his work; he was not in any way intimidated by the words of the Bishop. When he was a twenty-five year old student he had been courageous enough to declare the beginnings of his teachings in Rome. How could he possibly be afraid as a fifty-year-old man?

Years passed by, many winter and summer storms swept strong winds around the northwestern tower of the Frauenburg Cathedral. The book about the movements of the heavenly stars matured to ever-greater completeness. Indeed, the words of the Bishop had achieved nothing more than that Copernicus had become more careful. Never did he leave his papers anywhere. When he went across the land he hid them in his leather bag, which was never out of his sight. Only with his most trusted friends did he discuss the progress of his work and the discoveries that had become more clear and served the truth without a doubt. Neither fear nor threat, nor requests or command, could turn him from the path that he had chosen to follow ever since his days at the Cathedral School of Leslau. During that time he clearly recognized his destiny pointed to the stars. He knew that the world had followed Ptolemy's error and that he wanted to lead the way out of darkness into the bright light of truth.

In spite of his withdrawal into the tower room of Frauenburg, in spite of his silence, word went from city to city, from land to land, and across Europe:

"In the city of Frauenburg in Ermland, the Canon, Nikolaus Copernicus, has calculated a new teaching about the movement of the heavenly planets!"

In the lecture halls of universities his name was mentioned alongside the Egyptian Ptolemy and the Greek scholar Pythagoras. In the most well-known printing places in Mainz and Nuremberg, scholars asked if there was any publication by the Astronomer of Frauenburg. Copernicus received letters in his quiet abode from all over Europe and they all begged him to hand over his book for publication. Meanwhile Copernicus remained untouched by all the commotion around him.

"Not yet!" he said to himself as he sat at his calculations. He was still haunted by doubts and lack of certainty, and so he searched for new truths. In this way only parts of his insights reached the public ear.

Some people could not praise him enough; they admired his knowledge and felt deeply humble when they spoke about him. Others ridiculed him as a fool.

"Every child can see that it is the Sun that moves," they exclaimed laughingly, and with curled-up lips they mocked his name.

Meanwhile Copernicus sat and worked in his tower room. He regarded neither reverence nor ridicule. He asked for neither praise nor laughter. As the stars in the sky, high above the Earth, move on their untouchable path, so the opinions of people could not touch his hermitage. He measured, calculated and observed without paying any attention to what people thought or said about him.

Carnival rolled through Ermland with all its crazy manifestations. Men, women and children wore masks and danced in the streets and the squares. Music sounded from the taverns until the early morning hours. The wise Dr. Wilhelm Gnapheus from Elbing thought of a particularly funny prank. In one of the backrooms of a hidden tavern he huddled together with his friends, ßheads together, whispering their ideas to each other. Elbing was to have a parody such as the little town of Ermland had not seen for many years. Was there not a crazy Canon living in Frauenburg about whom so many strange things were spoken? Dr. Gnapheus demanded silence with a brief gesture of his right hand and revealed his plan to his friends. Repeatedly his words were interrupted by uncontrollable laughter. Men slapped their thighs and jumped up from their chairs, they were so shaken up by the fun they were having. Full of admiration and recognition, they patted the wise doctor on the shoulders and were still chuckling as they left the tavern late that night and began their unsteady walk home.

On the Monday before Lent Copernicus traveled in his heavy sleigh through Elbing. He had once again been entrusted with important business by the other Canons and was on his way home from the villages beside the lagoon. He thought that he would drink a glass of hot wine in one of the taverns in Elbing. The day had been a cold one and he wanted to travel towards Frauenburg with fresh horses. He wore his long, thick fur coat over his robe and could not be recognized by anyone. When he came to the market place the crowds were so thick that the driver had to halt the horses. He turned to Copernicus with a questioning gesture:

"Sir, we need to wait until the crowd has dispersed! It is the Monday before Lent, and Elbing has its yearly carnival parade! Shall I make a detour through the back alleys?"

"Drive the sleigh a little to the side and enjoy yourself with the people at their foolish games. When they have dispersed I will expect you at the southern city gate!"

Copernicus left the coach and mixed, unrecognized, with the people. Laughter came from behind magical masks. Unknown people took him by the arm and dragged him along the street for a while. It seemed as if the world had gone crazy. Everywhere there were excited onlookers and happy sightseers, from Castlegate to Drullishagen, from Saint Juergenpforte to the old parts of the city. Kettledrums and trumpets could be heard over-riding all the other noises; colorful masks wildly danced in the square. In its center there was a large scaffold. A foolishly dressed man tried to climb up the ladder while many voices acknowledged him with their screams:

"Doctor Gnapheus! Doctor Gnapheus!"

With a wide movement of the arms he stopped the shouting. Slowly it became quiet. All eyes were glued to this crazy man:

"People of Elbing! A new prophet has arisen in Frauenburg. He wants to convince us that the Earth is in movement while the Sun is not!"

Ripples of laughter interrupted his words. Necks stretched higher. In the back rows people stood on chairs and stools which they had brought with them in order to see more clearly.

"The comedy by the Prophet of Frauenburg!" shouted Gnapheus with a voice so shrill that it almost failed him.

Two strangely dressed figures danced out of a house into the square. A glaring gown shrouded one with golden rays, surrounding a masked face like a wreath. She held a sign in her hands on which was written the word "Sun" with shining letters. The other figure wore a long black gown and a donkey's head.

On the breastplate around her neck was "Earth" written in childlike lettering. With the strangest of contortions and awkward movements the "Earth" began to dance around the "Sun." Suddenly the "Sun" put her hand against her forehead it was as if she were pondering something difficult. Then she walked with solemn steps towards the motionless "Earth," stretched up her arms vertically into the air, and screamed:

"You have to dance around me, the Sun. The Canon in Frauenburg has commanded it!"

The "Sun" did not move to begin with but then slowly she began to walk and disappeared silently into the house, from which she reappeared a little later out of the dark entrance gate. She pulled a donkey on a long rope that had a board hanging around its neck. Written in thick, red letters was an inscription:

"I am Nikolaus Copernicus, the Prophet of Frauenburg!"

The music began to play a wild dance and the "Sun" pulled the donkey with crazy leaps all around the square. The people roared with laughter and screamed:

"Go on, dance! Go on, dance!"

Now the figure "Earth" in its long gown tried to jump onto the back of the donkey, but the donkey kicked with its hind legs, performed some wild jumps, and the "Earth" rolled onto the snow, got up with some difficulty and in pain held her hips and stomach. Then she disappeared into the entrance gate groaning.

Copernicus stood silently among the crowd while the laughter roared ever louder filling the square with an unruliness. He noticed how his hands began to shake, how everything around him began to sink into a whirling, misty fog. The screaming of the crazy people burned him like fire. With the last of his strength he forged himself a small pathway through the crowd. The laughter accompanied him and dragged his name into the mud. Slowly it became quieter as he staggered through the alleys to the southern gate.

Silently he climbed into the sleigh and requested with a tired gesture of the hand that the driver leave. Full of concern the driver turned to the Canon, whose pale face he had noticed:

"Is the Master not well?"

Copernicus tiredly shook his head and answered tonelessly:

"Just drive on. Drive as fast as you can, home to Frauenburg!"

The sleigh jerked, then glided over the deep snow. Soft, light flakes fell from the veiled gray sky and covered the world with a soft white cloth. The sleigh dashed through quiet villages. Slowly dawn rose above the horizon in the east. Copernicus touched his eyes with his hands. He thought that he felt a tear, but it was only a snowflake on his eyelashes.

A few days later Tiedemann stormed excitedly into the quiet, tower room with a glowing face.

"Have you heard what happened in Elbing the Monday before Lent?"

The Canon looked away from the papers for a moment upon which he was writing, and for a time put his pen aside.

"Please do not remind me of it, Tiedemann!" he begged.

"How did you know?"

"I saw everything with my own eyes!"

"You, yourself, were in Elbing?"

Copernicus merely nodded and picked up the pen again.

"You must lay charges on Gnapheus! You must take him to court, Nik!"

"No, Tiedemann! Let it be! One cannot force people to understand. They are blind. And—knowledge is grace, not given to everybody!"

Full of astonishment, his friend heard the calm, mature sentences.

"Knowledge is grace!" he repeated, thinking about it. After a while he flared up again:

"You are not going to do anything about it?"

"O yes, Tiedemann!"

"What?" asked the guest, full of trepidation. He had leaned so far forward that he could see deeply into the eyes of Copernicus.

"Work, Tiedemann! Work so that knowledge becomes ever clearer! Work so that those who are blinded now will perhaps one day, be able to see!"

The pages rustled and the pen glided over the paper in the quiet tower room. Softly Tiedemann left the room in a daze and climbed down the steep circular staircase.

"Knowledge is grace!" he whispered once more as he walked through the snow in the shadow of the Cathedral. The sky was clear as it arched over the landscape. The moon stood full and majestic between many stars.

10

DE REVOLUTIONIBUS

I n spring of the year 1539 a sea of blossoms had transformed
Ermland. Nikolaus Copernicus opened the locked windows of
his tower room in Frauenburg—wide, very wide. He breathed
deeply of the mild air that was carried on
the breeze into his room. The windows
had remained closed for a very long time;
now he enjoyed watching the red sails of
the boats dance up and down beside the
bank of the lagoon. He went over to his
table and put the big pile of papers in order. Carefully he placed one upon the
other upon the oak tabletop. One single
sheet still remained blank. He walked up
and down in the room a few times, then
took a blunt quill and drew with
celebratory lines the title that he wanted
to give to his work: *De Revolutionibus
Orbium Coelasticum.*

"Movements of the Heavenly Bodies!" he spoke quietly to
himself. From a tin can he took some fine sand and sprinkled it
over the letters so that they would dry more easily. He then placed
the title page on top of the high pile of papers that were full of
his small handwriting. With motherly tenderness he lovingly
stroked the papers as the sun's rays shone into his room and
playfully lit up the Canon's taught face where bones were begin-

ning to dominate the definition. His face was lined with many tiny wrinkles and folds, his hair was thinning and appeared golden in the sunlight. The Canon was getting old.

Outside the wheels of a dusty coach bumped along the uneven cobblestones of the Frauenburg road and came to a halt just before the northwestern tower. A young man in an elegant suit disappeared through the door and hurried up the winding stairway. A few moments later he stood in the entrance to the Canon's room. Copernicus looked at him questioningly and pointed to a high armchair near the window.

"I am George Joachim von Lauchen!" the guest introduced himself.

"From where?"

"Professor of Mathematics in Wittenberg. I am known there as Rheticus."

"From Wittenberg? From Martin Luther's city?" Copernicus asked in astonishment. After a little while he continued:

"I admire your courage. The new Bishop of Ermland, Danticus, is not on good terms with all those who follow the new teaching!"

Silently the guest bowed his head and responded in a whisper:

"Martin Luther also talks about you in an unpleasant way, Canon."

Copernicus shot up. He thought of that day when he had heard the name of the monk for the first time. Suddenly all the hope that he had felt towards his guest from Wittenberg dwindled.

"What has he said about me? Don't be afraid, you cannot offend me. I have become an old man. Life has matured me enough to bear this injustice as well."

For a while Rheticus hesitated, then he began to speak haltingly:

"At an evening dinner party I sat at Luther's table. We spoke about the art of Astronomy. Many names were mentioned. Then when yours came up Luther spoke: 'That fool in Frauenburg wants to create chaos in the whole sky!'"

From the walls of the tower the echo returned: "Fool!" The wind carried the word far into the countryside: "Fool!" The Canon shuddered as though a whip had lashed him. A deep disappointment showed on his face and made it appear even more pale and transparent. Calmness and silence hovered like a gray ghost between the two men, the Canon of the Catholic Church and the young Professor from Wittenberg, friend and supporter of Martin Luther.

"And yet you come to me?" Copernicus asked full of surprise. "You traveled to come see a fool?"

Rheticus jumped up from the armchair; falling over himself he knelt in reverence before the Canon taking his two hands in a firm grasp. He looked for words but the clasp of his fingers expressed everything that his voice could not. He stroked the wrinkled, veined hands, and he looked into the face that had slowly recovered color.

"I want to learn from you, Master!" the young guest whispered, and feeling ashamed he bowed his head and slowly returned to his chair covering his face with his hands. Copernicus looked at the Professor. He was youthful, full of life, eager to learn, and honest. His thoughts turned to his own experiences and went back far into his past where he came to rest at the years when he himself, just like this young Rheticus, sat at the feet of his professors. He thought of Leslau and of Krakow, of Bologna and Ferrara. He whispered the names of those who had taught and inspired him, who had stirred in him the flame of knowledge. Somewhere in this immeasurable yet tiny world these men lay, covered by soil.

He was deeply moved that a youth had come to him in order to learn, to absorb his wisdom, to complete and spread the truth from generation to generation, all so that it could become more and more illuminated and brighten the darkness of the earth.

Copernicus got up and with soft steps walked over to Rheticus who sat there still feeling ashamed. He lifted the face of the young Professor and stroked his thick, blonde hair with slightly trembling hands.

"Everything that I have managed to experience and learn in forty years I will share with you, Rheticus. That which I know you shall know too. Come!"

With slow, yet almost festive steps he led him to the table and showed him the different piles of his written papers.

"De Revolutionibus!" read Rheticus. The papers rustled as he turned them page by page. The wonderful world of Nikolaus Copernicus was revealed to the young Professor like a gift from God too vast for the human mind to grasp.

One night Rheticus sat in the small chamber that had been furnished for him next to Copernicus's room. A small candle cast its thin light onto the paper and the quill. Rheticus was bent over the table and writing a long letter to Martin Luther, a letter which revealed his admiration for the Astronomer.

> My teacher, Dr. Nikolaus Copernicus, has written six books which embrace the entire world of Astronomy. The first book gives a description of the cosmos, the second develops the teaching of the movement of the stars in the universe, and the third book deals with the Sun, which is at the center of the planets. In the fourth book he writes about the movement of the Moon and its eclipses, in the fifth he talks about the movement of all the remaining planets. The sixth book is a summary of the previous five.

These sentences Rheticus wrote in red ink and with special care for the lettering. After he had sealed the roll, the Canon came into the room. The morning sun shone through the window and cast a golden light on the entering, slightly bent figure. The Professor from Wittenberg looked at him as if he were an unearthly appearance. Both stood opposite each other without speaking a word. Then Copernicus read the inscription on the roll:

"Dr. Martin Luther? You write to him although he maintains that I create disorder in the sky? Oh, yes, he is right. I have overthrown it in my work. But I have not created chaos, rather given it its proper order."

"Master, give me your work. I will take it to Nuremberg so that it can be printed!"

The Canon lifted his arms as though he wanted to hold something back. Then he went into his room and took the papers bound in parchment into his hands, as if he had to protect them from every attempt to have them seized. Suddenly he was overwhelmed by fear of revealing his thoughts to the world.

Sincerely Rheticus pressed the hesitating man:

"Truth belongs to humanity! You cannot keep it to yourself!"

"And if it is not the truth? If the book contains mistakes?"

"I am convinced—and I feel it! It is the truth! Say yes, Master!"

Copernicus stroked the papers with trembling fingers. Thoughtfully, in a dreamy voice he spoke to himself:

"Forty long years have I spent on this work. It is a testament to lost sleep of many nights and also to the despair and inner struggle as to whether I would succeed. My life is coming to an end, and I have to account for this life—not only to God, but also before the world. So may the world judge my work and me. Rheticus, you, in all these years, are the only student who has fully understood me. I trust you with the book. Take care that the printer in Nuremberg does not change anything."

Copernicus let his fingers glide over the pages once more, then he placed the book slowly and hesitatingly into the hands of the young Professor. Copernicus turned quickly, and looking out of the window onto the landscape he spoke:

"Do not say another word and do not mention gratitude, Rheticus. I feel at this moment as if I am torn into two parts and have given you the more valuable one.

"I feel that you will take away with you the strength that has kept me alive, the strength that for me was connected to this book. But you are right: the world has a claim on the truth. And if the book contained only one single sentence of truth, it would be a sin to keep it to myself. Go now, go, Rheticus! I must be alone. And bring everything to a good end. I – trust – you – with everything – that I have owned!"

Tired, the Canon staggered over to the table, sat down in his armchair and let his head and arms drop. It seemed as if his shoulders were trembling with pain. With the book in his hands, Rheticus stood without moving, his lips opened to say something, but he remained silent and left the room quietly. Without noise he closed the door and soundlessly found his way down the winding stairs. He wanted to shout for joy but a fearful premonition sealed his lips. He thought that perhaps he had seen the Master for the last time. Outside he looked up to the high, gray walls of the tower. He searched the window under the red roof to catch a glimpse of the beloved figure and to send up one last grateful greeting. But he waited in vain. The familiar face remained hidden. Only black jackdaws sailed calmly around the brick walls and the immeasurable sky arched in deep blue over the quiet city.

Slowly Rheticus wandered across the square in front of the cathedral and turned towards the harbor from where the couriers were leaving. Firmly his hands grasped the parchment roll with its many pages. He felt as if he were carrying heaven and earth in his arms.

"His name is still missing on the first page!" he thought to himself. "I will have it printed with big letters: Nikolaus Copernicus!"

He began to walk faster. His forehead glowed as if he had a high fever, and his heart was ready to burst with the pride and joy he experienced. The waves of the lagoon's waters reached its banks and the wide ships rocked softly up and down. The bright sails shimmered red over the blue flood.

ဗ ဗ ဗ

It was lonely, ever more lonely for the Frauenburg Canon. Forgotten were the days whe he as Regent of Allenstein, had brought happiness into the houses of the people. Hardly anybody remembered the time when he had governed Ermland as General Administrator and spent all his strength and concern on the region. Rare was the guest who found his way up the winding steps into the tower room of the Astronomer. Rarely was the door opened. Sometimes in these long hours a feeling of bitterness crept up in him. Had the whole world forgotten him? Why did he not receive news from Nuremberg where his book was going to be printed? Could not Rheticus find time for even a short message to him? With a clenched jaw he looked at the clouds and stars, and it seemed to him as if the stars had lost some of their shine. Or had his eyes become so weak that all things seemed dull and gray? He felt superfluous on this earth and useless to anyone. Since the work that had taken him over forty years had been taken out of his hands all the joy of living had left him to be judged by the world.

His work! Sometimes he was overcome by fear that the printers far away in Nuremberg might deliberately falsify his results. At those times he came close to calling the servant to reserve a place on the fast coach. But he felt that his body had become too weak to endure such a long journey. He would take pen and paper to at least write a few lines to the printer in Nuremberg. However, when he would begin the first sentences, he worried that his worries could not be expressed in words because there were too many. With a sigh he would lay the pen aside and crumple up the paper on which he had written half a page. He had to let go of everything. He, who had subjected the heavenly bodies to his intellectual probing and study to reveal their secrets, had become powerless. The things of the world took their path, and Nikolaus Copernicus had merely become a wilted leaf in the wind. With no resistance he felt as if he were whirling through the universe. More often than before he thought of death; he had no fear and was ready for it as if it were a good friend.

Yet once more the old spirit awakened to a flame. An messenger had brought him an urgent letter from Rome. The name of the Eternal City awakened memories of years full of youthful strength and beauty, the day when he boldly delivered his daring lecture before the Academy, and the wonderful hours he had spent as guest in the palace of Goritz von Luxemburg. Hastily and full of apprehension and curiosity he tore open the seal and looked for the signature.

"Nikolaus Schoenberg, Cardinal of Capua," he read, and thought about the evening when the Cardinal was with him as a guest of Allenstein. Full of anticipation he scanned the lines.

"Nikolaus Schoenberg, Cardinal of Capua, greets Nikolaus Copernicus. I have heard that you have devised a new world order in which you teach that the Earth moves and that the Sun is in the center, that the Moon moves between Mars and Venus and in the course of one year circles around the Sun once. I have heard that you have completed a book about your entire astronomical wisdom. I have heard that you have calculated the planets. I beg you to send me this work!"

A few days later Copernicus handed to the courier big sealed rolls containing parts of his book. He followed the departing coach with his eyes for a long time as it rolled southward over the cobblestones of Frauenburg, along the well known road that passed Nuremberg and Augsburg, over the Brenner Pass to Bologna, always south to the Eternal City on the Seven Hills.

"My work is demanded in Rome!" he murmured, shaking his head repeatedly. He could not grasp that the Pope was interested in his work. Was he not thinking of him as a heretic who had dared to maintain an opposing view to what the Church had believed about the Earth, the Sun and stars? A secret glimmer of pride arose in him.

"Truth must find its own way sooner or later!" he thought and before his eyes appeared the picture of the beautiful Eternal City.

In the gardens of the Vatican, Pope Paul III sat in the shade of palm trees and enjoyed the cool, gurgling waters of a fountain. He dreamily engaged in the game of leaves which, cradled by the wind, drifted through the air, and he listened attentively to Nikolaus Schoenberg, Cardinal of Capua who read from a parchment that lay on his lap. Only once did he interrupt the Cardinal, and pointing with his hand, the golden fisher-ring sparkling for a moment on the book, he said:

"The Canon of Frauenburg has courage. I did not expect him to send excerpts of his work to Rome."

"He would certainly not have the courage were he not convinced that his teaching is correct!" the Cardinal responded and leafed through the pages.

The Pope got up from his reclining chair and began to walk among the flowers and bushes, out into a meadow from where he could survey the sea of Roman houses. He beckoned the Cardinal and pointed to the magnificent cupola of the new church of St. Peter:

"The name of Michelangelo will be connected forever to this cupola, and so, too, with this volume, the name of Nikolaus Copernicus. Only the most daring spirits transcend their lifetimes and influence the Earth as long as it exists."

In the afternoon sun the mighty cupola glistened high into the blue sky.

"The spirit of the people is stronger than we might have guessed!" the Pope spoke thoughtfully and returned to his shady place under the palm trees. Only in the last hours of the evening did Nikolaus Schoenberg close the book from which he had read to Paul III without pause. For a while longer the Pope remained in thought, and then he asked:

"What did the Bishop of Ermland write about the Frauenburg Canon?"

"He has asked a certain Hosius to watch over him. I also read in his letter that he wants to take Copernicus to court for heresy."

Slowly the Pope lifted his hand:

"Before the day is over a courier must be sent to Ermland to take my message. I will not have the Astronomer harmed in any way. Write my wish onto a piece of paper and give it to me for my signature. The thoughts of the Frauenburg Canon are great and daring, but perhaps our time is not yet ready to understand their depth!"

The cupola glowed purple-red in the evening sky and all eyes of the people looked spellbound at the dramatic, vaulted curvature. Slowly the Pope and his Cardinal walked through the fragrant park and the cool passages of the Vatican. During the same night an express messenger galloped his horse north as fast as it could go. The stars shimmered with a soft glow and pointed the way.

In Wittenberg on the Elbe, Rheticus tried in vain to change Martin Luther's opinion. With glowing words he told him about Ermland, with its dark forests and deep quiet lakes, of the red sails and the constant roaring of waves as they broke onto the coast. He read to the old former monk from the book of the Astronomer and told him about the many discussions he had had with Copernicus over the past two years. Luther was not swayed from his previously reached opinion.He opened the Bible that he had translated during the hard years on the Wartburg at Eisenach and read with a hard voice, full of anger:

"It says here the Earth is not to be moved unto eternity!"

Hastily he leafed through the pages of the Holy Book:

"The Earth stands in all eternity, the Sun rises and sets!"

Full of pain and compassion he looked at the young scholar who held the pages from Frauenburg firmly in his hands, and scolded him with sharp words:

"Did the Astronomer confuse you too, a Professor in Mathematics, in whom I had full confidence? For me he remains what he has always been, a fool who has brought the entire sky into disorder!"

And with a firm voice he began to sing the song that he had written:

"A solid fortress is our God!"

This song had given him strength at the time he was asked to recant his teachings in the city of Worms before the German parliament. This song would now strengthen him against the teachings of Nikolaus Copernicus. The mighty melody sounded throughout the room and reverberated from the walls like distant drumming.

ᛒ   ᛨ   ᛝ

Far in the south in Nuremberg, the towers of the Church of St. Lorenz reached high into the sky. A light shone from one of the rectory's windows that was built close to the church. The preacher, Andrew Osiander, sat over the engraving plates of the book by Nikolaus Copernicus that the master had brought to his workshop quite late the night before. "*De Revolutionibus!* By Nikolaus Copernicus," he read on the cover page.

Next to him on his desk lay the letter, which had reached him a few days earlier from Wittenberg, and in which Rheticus had asked him to supervise the printing of the work.

From that evening on he sat many days and nights over the four hundred and fifty pages written by the Frauenburg Astronomer. The more he got involved in the thought world of the book, the more clearly he perceived the bold ideas. But in the process of reading he became increasingly more fearful. He knew that Martin Luther called Copernicus a fool who had brought the entire sky into disorder. Osiander himself was a faithful advocate of Luther's teaching whose beliefs he had preached himself and had helped to bring to victory in Nuremberg.

How could he dare to print a book which made these foolish ideas available to the whole world? He became restless and lost sleep. He thought this way and that of how he could resolve the conflict before him. One thing was clear: he could not touch the work itself. Chased and tormented he blundered through the streets of Nuremberg; he stood at the Kaiser's castle and looked far into the Franconian landscape before he returned again to his study.

It was on a rainy night that he jumped out of his bed upon which he had been restlessly tossing and turning without sleep. The storm howled around the house and the window shutters flapped noisily against the brick walls. Hastily he turned on the light, went to get a pen and paper and began to write. Disheveled, his uncombed hair hanging across his forehead, his eyes flickering restlessly like the candle, he wrote feverishly. Occasionally he stopped to reread what had just entered his head. The morning dawned before he read through the lines one final time. For some sentences his voice became quite loud and sounded empty and hollow through the cold room:

"I have no doubt that many scholars will be quite shocked when they read that the Earth moves and the Sun is fixed in the middle of the universe. One would hope that science would not enter into confusion... It is not necessary to believe that the assumptions in this book are true...."

He nodded with satisfaction, placed his three pages into a folder, put a rain cape over his shoulders and walked past the Church of Saint Lorenz, through the small alleyway towards the main market place. He turned into a narrow side path and knocked at the printer's door. In the stillness of the morning the banging could be heard all around. It took a while before the sleepy head of the master looked out of the top window of the upper story, annoyed at the disturbance.

"You, Osiander? At this early hour you come to me?"

"Open the door! I have brought you important pages!"

Moments later the door was opened with a squeak and Osiander entered the workshop and smelled the black printer's ink.

"How far have you come with the Astronomer's book?"

"Fifty pages have been printed, one hundred are ready to go to the press!"

From under his cape Osiander brought out the folder and withdrew the three pages. Hastily he pressed them into the hands of the printing master:

"These three pages you must enter just after the title page, they need to be seen before the first chapter of the opus."

"A foreword, I take it?" asked the printer.

"You could call it so," Osiander confirmed. Then he left the workshop with a superficial farewell. The printer shook his head as he looked after the preacher. Osiander walked through the slowly awakening city of Nuremberg. The farm ladies had begun to set up their vegetable stalls around the Frauenburg church. The tip of the small fortress tower was covered in golden sunrays. The preacher breathed a sigh of relief. It was as if a heavy burden had fallen from his shoulders and yet he could not be happy. Depressed he sneaked through the alleys, and the peace for which he had searched did not enter into his heart. Again and again he had thought about the introductory sentences that were now in the hands of the printer. Did he not, with these, give a totally different meaning to the Astronomer's work? Was it not falsifying the clear results of years of research by Copernicus? He mumbled a curse for Rheticus who had brought him this book and asked him to be its guardian. It was a wretched task. He shivered and wrapped himself more securely in his dark cloak. Deep clouds hung around the towers of Saint Lorenz.

Meanwhile Copernicus lived alone in his tower room in Frauenburg. He knew nothing of what was happening in Rome, not even that his work was being printed in Nuremberg, as Rheticus, too, had wrapped himself in silence. He thought constantly about his book. After all, he had dedicated his life to it. Only rarely did he pick up a pen because everything that he could research with his mind was already in these four hundred and fifty pages. He felt pride, yet he remained humble. As time passed he experienced more and more a secret fear that the Church would ban his book.

In a quiet evening hour he had the idea that he could dedicate the opus to Pope Paul III and so he began to write down on a few pages what he felt:

"I am fully conscious, Holy Father, that when some people realize that in my books I attribute a certain movement to the

Earth, they will say that such teaching is objectionable.... For this reason I was at a loss as to whether I should let the explanations and proofs of these movements come to light.... My friends alone brought me to the point of reaching the decision to publish the book, among them Nikolaus Schoenberg, Cardinal of Capua, and Tiedeman Giese, Bishop of Culm. The latter often urged, even pressed me with the request, to allow my work to be seen by the public. But I kept the book with me— not only nine years but four times nine years. I ask you, Holy Father, to protect me from calumny. If thoughtless slanderers will criticize my work, I will not pay attention to them but rather pity them!"

The foreword, which Copernicus had written for his book's journey into the world, arrived on the Preacher's writing desk only a few days later. Andrew Osiander sat in his study in the little house close by the Lorenz church in Nuremberg. He held the papers in trembling hands, but he did not carry them to the printer. He locked them into a strong chest in the furthest corner of his room. For the second time he was a traitor to the work of the great Astronomer.

Rarely did Copernicus leave his tower room, but one beautifully sunny day, he gave in to a secret longing to revisit his birthplace in Torun. His servant guided the horses carefully over the streets of Ermland trying to avoid the potholes and other uneven bumps on the country roads. The coach arrived by the Northgate on a beautiful Sunday. Copernicus wore a red robe with a white, fur collar. The cap covered his very thin, light hair. A sword at his side Nikolaus Copernicus marched as a nobleman through the familiar streets and alleys of Torun. For a long time he stood thoughtfully before the little house in St. Anne's Alley. He did not know any of the strange people who were going in and out of the gateway. He wandered around the mighty tower of St. John's Church and crossed the market place. To the south lay the house in which he had grown up. He walked close to the wall and looked in the open windows.

Everything had changed; he did not know the furniture or the people. He was overcome with sadness and with hasty steps hurried towards the Vistula. Wide and powerful streamed the river along its path. In the harbor lay the ponderous boats, their names in white lettering: "*Danzig,*" he read. "*Hanse, Sea-God, Hamburg, Mariah,*" and—*Silesia.*" Joy welled up in him when he saw the last name. He stepped closer to the thick ropes that anchored the ship. Like a young rascal, the almost seventy-year-old man whistled the tune that long ago was meant for old Kirsten. He had not forgotten its tune, but it was a quiet, uncertain whistle that came across his lips, and among the figures that walked up and down the deck of the ship he could not find Kirsten. As he came closer to the harbor wall he recognized that it was no longer the old "*Silesia*" which rocked up and down on the waves, but was a new ship that simply bore the familiar name. Slowly Copernicus wandered back to the city. He spoke to no one; he was accompanied only by the memories which had arisen in him in the most powerful way. They stayed with him the entire way from Torun to Frauenburg. When he stepped out of the coach and climbed the winding stairs with great difficulty, he knew that this was a farewell to his beloved life. It had driven him on this trip with such force that he had not been able to resist. Now he felt how everything was slipping out of his hands: the city in which he had grown up, the people, his life's work, and all the strength with which he had served his task for almost seventy years.

ᛒ   ᛦ   ᛥ

May of 1543 blossomed with extravagant beauty around the northwestern tower. Copernicus did not see the satisfying heavenly blue and did not breathe in the sweet scent of flowers. The window was tightly covered and the sunlight fell only faintly through the colorful curtains. Tired, unbelievably tired, he rested on his bed. The angle and the measuring instruments hung on the wall, but his hands did not have the strength to grasp them. The oak surface of the table lay empty and the ink in the quill had dried up. Quietly the sand seeped through the hourglass funnel. Somewhere outside birds sang in the trees.

A rider on a sweating horse galloped into Frauenburg. At the small door of the tower the old Tiedeman Giese received him. He took the book with trembling hands, and the rider spoke:

"Rheticus gave me the task to bring this to you. 'Change your horses four times,' he said to me. 'But ride so fast that you beat death!' Six horses collapsed under me!"

Tiedeman heard the hidden question.

"He is still alive, friend!" he said. Then he opened the book quickly:

"*De Revolutionibus!*" he read, and louder:

"Nikolaus Copernicus, Canon and Astronomer from Frauenburg." His trembling fingers turned the pages. His eyes drew together to form narrow slits. A deep frown grew vertically upon his forehead. Fury burned blood red in his face.

"No, Osiander! No!" he screamed with a hoarse voice. Then his hands tore out three pages and crumpled them with holy anger. Full of astonishment the messenger observed this puzzling act of the old man.

"They want to falsify his work! No! Never ever will they be allowed to succeed!"

He stumbled up the stairs and entered the room. The canons that stood around the Astronomer's bedside quietly made room for him. High up he held the book in his hands and step by step he approached the bed. At the bedside he fell on his old, weak knees and laid the book into the pale and motionless hands.

"Nik, your book! It has just arrived from Nuremberg. It is complete!"

With a very slow motion, Copernicus turned his head to the side. His hands closed with hardly perceptible pressure around the many pages. He whispered:

"It is complete!" His voice spoke haltingly and with great effort. A shimmer of the deepest joy passed over his pale, haggard face.

"It – is – complete!" he repeated once more, almost inaudible. Then his head fell forward with a sudden jerk.

"He is dead!" someone said quietly in the room.

In the silence of the room the word sounded awful. Tiedeman stood up and stretched to his full size, wide and large his eyes looked out of his glowing face:

"Dead? No, a man like Nikolaus does not die! He lives. He lives – in – his – work!"

With infinite reverence he fumbled for the hands of the silent Astronomer and folded the cold fingers around the golden parchment. One of the Canons went to the window and pulled the curtains back. With blinding brightness the light of the sun flooded in from the blue sky. Its radiant beams lit up the decorative letters of the top page:

"*De Revolutionibus!* Nikolaus Copernicus, Canon and Astronomer from Frauenburg."

On the table, the calendar showed May 24, 1543. The large bell of the cathedral sounded heavy tones into the blossoming landscape. Many people heard the sounds and said to each other:

"Someone has died!"

The spring of life is stronger than all death. The birds sang, and the flowers blossomed. The Sun stood with her golden rays in the sky and the waves rolled onto the beach of Frauenburg.

Important Dates

1471   The birth of Albrecht Dürer

1473   Nikolaus Copernicus is born on February 17th in Torun

1477–89   Veit Stoss creates the altar of Saint Mary in Krakow.

1487   Bartholomew Diaz sails around the Cape of Good Hope.

1491–94   Copernicus studies at the University of Krakow.

1492   Columbus's first voyage

1495   Copernicus studies in Bologna.

1497   Acceptance into the Church Registry of Ermland

1498   Savonarola was burned at the stake. Vasco da Gama finds the sea passage to India. Third journey for Columbus

1500   Copernicus in Rome

1503   Promotion in Ferrara

1505   First mail service between Brussels and Vienna

1506–12   Copernicus becomes Counselor to the Bishop in Heilsberg.

1507   Copernicus completes his treatise *De Revolutionibus Orbium Coelasticum*

1509–10   Works by Erasmus Encomium Moriae and Institutio Christiani Principis

1510   Peter Henlein invents the pocket watch.

1512   Copernicus moves to Frauenburg.

1514   Machiavelli's *Il Principe* is published.

1516–20   Copernicus becomes Regent of Allenstein.

1517   Beginning of Martin Luther's Reformation in Wittenberg
First coffee imported to Europe

1519–20   Cortez conquers Mexico.

1520   Ferdinand Magellan sails the Pacific Ocean.
Luther burns the Bannbulle.

1521   Imperial Day at Worms

1523   Copernicus becomes General Administrator of the Diocese.

1525   Prussian State becomes Western Dukedom.

1528   Albrecht Dürer dies.
The cocoa bean comes to Europe.

1541   The medical doctor Theophrastus
Paracelsus dies.

1543   Copernicus dies on May 24th in
Frauenburg. His book *De Revolutionibus
Orbium Coelasticum* appears in print.
Prohibition of Indian slavery
Hartmann in Nuremberg discovers the in-
clination of the magnetic needle.

1757   *De Revolutionibus* taken off the *Index* of
banned books in the Catholic Church